WARFARE IN THE HOME

EMPOWERING WOMEN OF COLOR AGAINST DOMESTIC VIOLENCE

Sonia Martin

ISBN 979-8-89428-839-0 (paperback)
ISBN 979-8-89428-840-6 (digital)

Christian Faith Publishing
832 Park Avenue
Meadville, PA 16335
www.christianfaithpublishing.com

Printed in the United States of America

This book is dedicated to my beloved son, David Michael. You are my heart and a gift from God to me. Greatness is in you. I love you. I also dedicate this book to my mother, the late Icilda May Martin (formerly Stewart). Thank you for your unconditional love and for standing by me during some of the darkest periods of my adult life.

It is the place where dreams end, and nightmares begin.
It is the world of Intimate Partner Violence (IPV).
—Mallika Nawal, Scholar and Lawyer

This book seeks to contribute to the overall intellectual and social understanding of intimate partner violence, employing the intersectionality of gender inequality and male oppression as they relate particularly to abused Black women. The author critically analyzes the attitude of Black church leadership toward victims of domestic violence.

The author, in acknowledging the role of the Black women as a stabilizing force for family and community, also boldly situates her predicament within the context of the domestic and sexual exploitation of the era of slavery in the United States, in addition to the well-established patriarchal tendencies that have been entrenched in human societies since the early ages.

Ultimately, in using this book to capture the anguish and the physical and psychological trauma of victims and survivors of domestic violence, the author not only helps them find their voice to reclaim their dignity, she also empowers abused Black women by drawing awareness to their plight and announcing her intention to facilitate both therapeutic workshops for victims and training workshops for all concerned stakeholders on how to identify and manage all aspects of intimate partner violence.

Contents

Foreword

t has been an absolute delight knowing Minister Sonia Martin. What started as an introduction through a mutual church friend has blossomed into a friendship nurtured by reciprocal respect and sincere affection, even as she pursued her doctorate in ministry. Minister Sonia Martin has been intentional about ensuring that the stories of victims of domestic violence are heard. Not only is she enthusiastic about raising awareness of domestic violence, but she does so in spaces where the conversation is not always comfortable.

In this book, Minister Sonia Martin explores the taboo topic of domestic violence in the African American church community. As a victim of domestic violence herself, she employs her experiences to explore the factors that influence and contribute to the continued cycle of domestic violence within the African American church community. Her riveting story, and that of other women, paints the poignant picture of the painful and silent torture that is hidden in plain sight within Black church communities across the United States.

Utilizing the dual perspectives of psychology and theology, Minister Sonia Martin delves into misconceptions about masculinity, the seemingly accepted marginalization of women, and the negative impact that these misguided theories have had on society, especially among intimate partners.

This book will help you assess your preconceived notions about domestic violence and how you can become an agent of empowerment in breaking the cycle. The church is traditionally seen as a refuge or place of safety. Yet within this valid context, many victims of domestic abuse have been turned away, dismissed, or made to feel that their truth does not matter. Empathy and nonjudgmental approaches are critical in creating an environment to which victims of domestic abuse can turn for support and safety.

This all-important book, *Warfare in the Home: Empowering Women of Color Against Domestic Violence*, provides readers with tangible resources to support victims and their families, as well as a template for training church leaders to effectively identify and respond to the needs of victims. In applauding the author for a timely and well-written book, I also sincerely commend the book to you.

Happy reading!

Cornelia R. Gilpin, DNP, RN, NEA-BC, CCSS

ACKNOWLEDGMENTS

acknowledge my struggle. This book could never have been written if I had not gone through the fire of experiencing firsthand as a victim and survivor of intimate partner violence at the hands of an abusive ex-husband. The process of writing this book brought back those painful memories, allowing me to do some deep reflection and uncover many things about myself.

I have always been attracted to men who I considered to have some form of power, be it intellectual power. Well, I met a man with a combination of intellect and money, but often some of these powerful men are more self-centered and much more dominant in nature. He was an extremely abusive man who, on many occasions, tried to kill me because of his unfounded jealousy. After his arrest for almost killing me, the senior pastor at his church expressed anger at my having my ex-husband arrested. I was left totally confused and hurt.

My traumatic experience led me to seek professional help. Ultimately, I found my strength and reclaimed my power to move forward with my life, with a mission to help other women who have suffered at the hands of intimate partners as I have.

I recognize that there are many young sisters who are patiently waiting in churches for a "saved" husband. I ask them to beware because abusers come in all forms. Abusers come dressed up in suits. They can be found in various types of professions. Sadly, many abusers are in church leadership, including pastors and Bible teachers at Sabbath Schools. They are singing in church choirs. Most importantly, perpetrators can be found behind the pulpit preaching at Sunday divine services. I encourage my sisters to walk in the Spirit, be spiritually discerning, and choose wisely.

The scripture says, "For I know the plans I have for you," declares the Lord, "plans to prosper you and not to harm you, plans to give you hope and a future" (Jeremiah 29:11 NIV). I decided to fully follow the plan of God for my life in 2016 when I attended New York Theological Seminary and obtained a master's in pastoral care and counseling, thus paving the way for my journey in pursuit of a doctorate in ministry at Northeastern Seminary. I never would have completed a doctoral program without the grace and mercy of God, and for this, I give God all the praise.

Today, I have chosen to take another step in faith in complete obedience to the calling of God in my life. God gave me the instruction to tell my story! The journey has been long and complex with many nights of burning the candle, but I did it. My conceptual understanding has increased, and I am enormously thankful for the learning process. The process of writing my dissertation for my doctorate in ministry, which I decided to convert into this book, has been a remarkably humbling experience. This process, I found to be a very challenging task, but the fruit of my labor is well worth the effort. I believe that the knowledge and enlightenment that I have obtained from my painful life experience in an intimate partner violent marriage have equipped me for the mission of providing encouragement, empathy, and empowerment to other women who are also struggling silently with domestic violence.

I am grateful for the support of my church family, my prayer line sisters: Verna, Mbonya, Minister Beverly, Elder Wanda, and Donna. To all those individuals who provided much-esteemed assistance and were in my corner cheering me on during my doctoral studies, I also would like to thank everyone who made invaluable contributions to this book. I would like to express my sincere gratitude to Pastor Walker and Pastor Turner, former pastors at the North Bronx Seventh-Day Adventist Church, for their emotional support and prayers during one of the most difficult times of my life. To my beloved son, David Michael, I say, "Thank you for your love, support, and encouragement."

The Anatomy of Intimate Partner Violence

It is the place where dreams end, and nightmares begin.
It is the world of Intimate Partner Violence (IPV).
—Mallika Nawal, scholar and lawyer

The World Health Organization (WHO) describes *intimate partner violence* as behaviors by an intimate partner or ex-partner that cause physical, sexual, or psychological harm, including physical aggression, sexual coercion, psychological abuse, and controlling behaviors. For the avoidance of confusion, intimate partners are individuals who have an intimate personal relationship. This means an *intimate partner* refers to a person who has a close relationship with emotional connectedness, regular contact, continuous physical contact, or sexual activity within the home.

The prevalence of intimate partner violence against women and girls, as evidenced by the consistent patterns and incidences of emotional abuse, sexual assault, physical battering, oppressive treatment, and premeditated murder committed by husbands or boyfriends, has approached disturbing, if not alarming, proportions. The National Center for Injury Prevention and Control (NCIPC) of the Centers for Disease Control (CDC) states that "over 1 in 5 women (22.3%), and nearly 1 in 7 men (14.0%), have experienced severe physical violence by an intimate partner at some point in their lifetime, translating to nearly 29 million US women." To say that countless women have survived unspeakable abuse at the hands of their partners would be merely stating the obvious. Many women have been dispatched to an early grave, while even more still exist in harrowing circumstances of unrelenting emotional distress, undignified physical debasement, and altogether a vicious cycle of psychological trauma. These acts of violence are found in homes, schools, and the workplace. Worse, institutions of religious practice, like the African American church, and higher citadels of learning are not spared this ugly endemicity.

Violence against women is not localized to the United States. As a worldwide phenomenon, it is the intentional disregard, exploitation, ill-treatment, and maltreatment of females by their male partners. Elizabeth L. Gerhardt, a doctor of theology with extensive background in theology, church history, and social ethics, wrote in her widely acclaimed book *The Cross and Gendercide: A Theological Response to Global Violence Against Women and Girls*, "Violence against women and girls is a human rights problem that impacts the lives of millions of families and communities." She is right. Furthermore, atrocious violence committed against women has become the norm in many cultures. Daily, women and girls are subjected to verbal intimidation, sexual attack, and physical assault, most often at the hands of men who ought to be their protectors. Indeed, even before matrimonial vows are uttered, many of these men have already begun unleashing their acts of terror on their spouses, girlfriends, or paramours. Although violence against women is a global phenomenon, there is a common denominator: the *male dominance mindset.*

Practically every day, there are stories of women who were physically victimized by husbands or boyfriends. However, I never once thought that this would happen to me. From talking about my experience in groups, I discovered that there were many church women who had silently suffered with Christian husbands. I became aware that there were many women who attend church yet go home to their abusive husbands. Within our churches, many hear about domestic violence but lack the understanding of what domestic violence is like for victims. Domestic violence is rooted in power and control, frequently through the use of fear and intimidation. Regularly, there is a pattern, which includes threats. For example, an abusive husband threatens to report his wife, who is an illegal immigrant, to the immigration services. An abusive spouse may use physical violence by hitting, punching, or even attempting to strangle the other spouse, thereby instilling fear within his partner. In most cases, at the beginning of the relationship, an abuser will associate jealousy with love. A man who is a persecutor will attribute his controlling behavior to being overly concerned for his girlfriend or wife. Leading any abusive man to question his wife about who she was with, he has the need to know every detail of his spouse's daily activities, he will check her cell phone. Then he makes unfounded accusations. He becomes easily jealous of her, begins to verbally belittle her, and/or physically assaults the woman he promised to love and cherish.

The crucial question then becomes, *why do men believe that masculinity is synonymous with power and control?* Australian theologian Shane Clifton, in his article "Spirit, Submission, Power, and Abuse: A Response to Teaching on Female Submission and the Scourge of Domestic Violence," argues, "The issue at stake is one of power, since enablement and concealment are the products of power… And the problem for some sections of the church is that their teaching and structures are overwhelmingly oriented to buttress the power of men and to disempower women." I will refer to Elizabeth L. Gerhardt again. She points out that early church history suggests that the prevailing belief system of male dominance contributed to the vilification of women. In fact, she articulates that "negative attitudes toward women have roots in early Christian teachings." On my part, I suggest that it is not only the culture and governing authorities that have maintained an oppressive system of permitting the belief that women and girls are inferior to boys and men. Unfortunately, the modern-day church has also played a role in sustaining the culture of oppression as it relates to women. Religious teaching has helped to further embolden and empower churchmen to perpetuate the belief that they are superior to women. Consequently, for most Black church women, there is a strong correlation between exposure to violence in the home, cultural programming, and a male-dominant society. Ultimately, tyranny against females is now almost considered the norm.

My aim with this book is to contribute to the overall intellectual and social understanding of intimate partner violence in the lives of women of color, their families, and their communities. I have, as much as possible, attempted to employ the intersectionality of race, class, gender, inequality, and oppression as these factors relate particularly to abused African American women. I have also strained myself to critically analyze the stance of Black church leadership toward victims of intimate partner violence by contrasting the prevailing culture within the church with biblical concepts on the issue. Jane Coaston, a former resident fellow at the University of Chicago's Institute of Politics, was once the host of the popular podcast *The Argument*. In agreeing with her, I intend to be brutally frank. Any attempt to understand the African-American female must begin with slavery because her existence in the United States was conceived and defined in that context. In slavery, black women were treated as breeders and satisfiers of white men's lust. They were property. Sexual exploitation shaped their lives during and after the period of slavery. Today, while female subordination and male dominance are central concerns of Black women, poverty, exclusion, and powerlessness are crucial issues for them. Yet despite the obstacles they confront, African American women remain a stabilizing force for their families, their communities, and society.

In the course of writing this book, I attempted to capture the experiences of victims and survivors of intimate partner violence. It was also an opportunity for them to verbalize their anguish, psychological trauma, and physical pain. In most cases, I left feeling that I somehow helped them find their voice and reclaim their equilibrium. With each passing encounter, I also left with the conviction that the issue of domestic violence has been a continuing and pervasive problem facing women from all cultural backgrounds, ethnicities, educational levels, and economic statuses. Furthermore, domestic violence greatly impacts women from the African American community and desperately needs to be addressed and effectively resolved. Not only do I aim to add to the current literature on the subject of intimate partner violence, but I also desire to create an empowerment program for abused women, including Black church sisters, with the ultimate objective of ameliorating their condition by drawing awareness to their belittling and degradation. Overall, I intend to facilitate therapeutic workshops for victims, promote domestic violence awareness, and offer training on how to identify the red flags and other warning signs of intimate partner violence.

I will be reviewing the contributory factors and consequences of domestic violence among women of color and its treacherous consequences. Power is a sociological phenomenon, and I will be examining its role and its coercive dynamics in an abusive relationship, especially how its misapplication impacts the relationships of Black women. In this narrative, I will make a bold attempt to provide Black church leadership with valuable information, effective tools, and resources that will enable them to be more proactive in managing domestic violence within their congregation. In due regard, I will be proposing church leadership educational training and workshops to provide tools that will enable them to be more effective in managing issues related to family violence. I will not spare the patriarchal mindset and cultural tendencies that contribute to intimate partner violence, since it is this mindset that has totally disoriented men to subject their women to abuse, mistreatment, and maltreatment.

I made a few assumptions in the course of my research into the subject of intimate partner violence. First, I assumed that pastors were sufficiently educated on safety procedures to provide counseling to abused women on how to secure themselves and their children. To my utter dismay, however, this assumption was invalidated when a senior pastor in the church advised me to remain in an abusive marriage despite his awareness of the dangerous and physically harmful nature of my untenable circumstances.

Secondly, I assumed that I could gain real-life insight into intimate partner violence by listening to the poignant narratives of Black church women who had suffered intimate partner verbal, psychological, and physical abuse and had survived to tell their stories. I believed this would afford me a greater amount of flexible approach in arriving at qualitative findings based on empirical data.

Thirdly, I assumed that I would be able to engage a sufficient number of African American abused women who had found a place of safety and/or are survivors of intimate partner violence. I certainly prayed that such women would be willing to openly and honestly express intimate details of their horrific experiences, especially since I was also determined to pay particular attention to their body language in nonverbal communication, including gestures, lack of eye contact, and facial expressions.

Based on those assumptions, my goal gradually evolved into providing educational resources for the African American church and educating pastors, women, and other members of the congregation about the reality of domestic violence and the unique considerations and solutions needed to address it. In this book, I will delve headlong into how the glaring lack of involvement and inconsistency in support of women by African American church leaders have had a devastating impact on Black families, despite the outsized role that African American women play in the overall stability of African American families.

It is no hidden fact that many Black men have abandoned their families for a constellation of reasons, leaving Black women with the burden of caring for the household alone and being the fulcrum on which the family stands. I am firmly convinced that there is a need for African American church leadership to affirm Black women's equality, the vital role they play, and their collective intrinsic human value.

I have had to ask many pertinent questions in the course of this work. Such questions included the following:

- What are some of the experiences of Black church women with intimate partner violence relationships?
- What are the key societal factors contributing to the disempowerment of Black women?
- How have church leaders helped to bring domestic violence awareness to the African American church community?

- In what ways can the African American church provide pastoral care and counseling, emotional support, and resources to victims of intimate partner violence?
- How has the cultural background and religious mindset of abused Black women contributed to their experience with intimate partner relationships?
- In what ways have African American church leaders helped facilitate the healing process and empowerment of abused Black women?
- How can African American church leaders more effectively address the problem of domestic violence in Black families and its impact on the lives of abused women and their children?

The intellectual effort that went into this book was no mean feat. Nothing was more challenging than attempting to unravel the most effective means of empowering African American abused women. I knew the best tools at my disposal would be *educational workshops* and *faith-based programs*. In basic conception, these programs will give women the freedom to express themselves and speak freely about all those conditions that might be an encumbrance of their rights to self-expression.

I have devoted exhaustive study to current theological thought, church leadership attributes, and the benefits to the community when pastors and church leadership are trained effectively to identify, address, and support women who suffer domestic cruelty, and I am convinced that the entire exercise has yielded its value in gold.

Once again, I wish you happy reading.

A Global Overview of Domestic Violence

> Domestic violence causes far more pain than the
> visible marks of bruises and scars. It is devastating to
> be abused by someone that you love and think loves
> you in return. It is estimated that approximately
> 3 million incidents of domestic violence are
> reported each year in the United States.
>
> —Dianne Feinstein,
> Democratic senator of the United
> States of America (1992–2023)

Permit me to open this book by stating clearly that I hold the firm conviction that no season is as ripe and as timely as this to address the issue of domestic violence. I write this book to confront this issue directly, seeking to provide insights and vital understanding into the experience of African American women who have somehow managed to survive violence on the domestic front.

Although the terms *domestic violence* (DV) and *intimate partner violence* (IPV) are often used interchangeably, intimate partner violence (IPV) is a mere subset of the broader evil of domestic violence (DV).

In this *introduction*, I will attempt an intellectual analysis of domestic violence as a necessary and foundational prelude to a more direct introduction to the subject of intimate partner violence in the *preface* that follows.

First, in the context of the subjects that I will discuss in this book, it is pertinent to offer definitions of those core subjects. The Center for Family Justice defines *domestic abuse* as "a pattern of coercive, controlling behavior that is a pervasive life-threatening crime affecting people in all our communities regardless of gender, age, sexual orientation, race, ethnicity, religion, social standing, and immigration status." On the other hand, the American Center for Disease Control (CDC) defines *intimate partner violence* (IPV) as "abuse or aggression that occurs in a close relationship," with *intimate partner* referring to both current and former spouses and dating partners.

IPV can vary in its frequency of occurrence and its severity. It can range from just one episode of violence that could have a lasting impact to a state of chronicity that involves several severe episodes lasting many years. The World Health Organization (WHO) helps to further dissect intimate partner violence into "physical, psychological, or sexual harm to those in the relationship." Examples of types of behavior include the following:

- Acts of physical violence, such as slapping, hitting, kicking, and beating
- Sexual violence, including forced sexual intercourse and other forms of sexual coercion
- Emotional (psychological) abuse, such as insults, belittling, constant humiliation, intimidation (e.g., destroying things), threats of harm, and threats to take away children.
- Controlling behaviors, including isolating a person from family and friends; monitoring their movements; and restricting access to financial resources, employment, education or medical care."

This book is not written to celebrate intimate partner violence, nor is it written to titillate the senses as a form of entertainment.

While, admittedly, it is a very interesting subject matter, and certainly one that occupies a prominent place in the social space of America, it is a subject that not only troubles society as a whole but also troubles the mental health of that society. Therefore, I have written this book not only to delve deeply into the subject but also to proffer solutions.

Indeed, while I sometimes employ my own story and experiences as eloquent references within the ambit of a wider, all-encompassing narrative, my overall objective is to empower abused Black women against domestic violence. The next pertinent definition I will offer is of the all-important word *empowerment.* In 1995, Gutierrez, DeLois, and Glen Maye offered what is now considered a classic definition of *empowerment.* They wrote, "*Empowerment* is the process of increasing personal, interpersonal, or political power so that individuals, families, and communities can take action to improve their situations." If writing exhaustively on intimate partner violence and then suggesting ways in which Black women can empower themselves against it, I would have achieved my objective.

The CDC reports that 4 million women each year are victims of violence perpetrated by men who have vowed to love, honor, and cherish them. Of more tragic coloration, approximately 1,200 women will be killed every year by those same men. I join thousands of fellow women workers in this field to declare that, regardless of the reasons for the violence visited upon women, there can be no rational justification for any man to lay his hands on any woman. Sadly, and according to Doris Williams Campbell and her coworkers, "*Femicide,* the killing of women, is also most often perpetrated by current or former husbands or boyfriends." Most victims of intimate partner violence have endured immeasurable acts of intimidation, in which the abuser instills fear in them. Abused women have suffered unspeakable emotional and physical assaults. The abused wife is, more often than not, totally overwhelmed with fear and self-blame, thinking she is bringing shame to her family as well as her church. Naturally, this creates a vicious and brutal cycle of violence, even as the woman continues to suffer in silence.

I am a Christian minister who has had the privilege of functioning in several positions in the church. For this reason, it is to be expected that I will make copious references to experiences in the church. Violence is everywhere. It is in educational institutions, even in close-knit church communities, and more importantly, it is happening in the privacy of homes. According to *Webster's Dictionary*, the definition of *home* is "one's place of residence; domicile; house." It is a place where children ought to live and thrive in a happy family environment. The home is where we were first taught how to pray to a loving God, and it is the place where children laugh and play. The home is the place where individuals feel that they belong. It is where we are most comfortable, having a sense of peace and unspeakable joy within the family environment. However, when there is domestic violence in the home, there is no love or peace. All of that is replaced with feelings of pain, misery, and agony. It is a place where dreams are made or promises are broken. The home is also where children learn how to interact and resolve conflicts appropriately or through acts of physical hostility. Violence is taught in homes where there is a culture of disrespect and abnormal, aggressive problem-solving.

There are numerous women and children who have experienced or are still suffering from the deadly experiences of severe forms of domestic violence. I draw attention to the fact that the inactivity, if not even seeming impotence, of church leadership has been enabled by certain faith-based traditions and biblical misrepresentations and misconceptions that have contributed to the oppression of women. There appears to be a lack of understanding on the part of some church leadership as it relates to the biblical perspectives on abusive relationships. It is my personal experience that, on several occasions, wives seeking spiritual guidance soon discover that they get insufficient support from church leaders. Naturally, this inadequacy in support from church leadership has resulted in distrust on the part of such abused women. That is why this book will also address the critical need and importance for church leadership to respond proactively and appropriately to reports of abuse by women. Indeed, there is a compelling need for Black church leaders and the church community to offer timely, nonjudgmental, and empathetic responses to abused women. I seek to emphasize that the dilemma of domestic violence visited on women is not just a serious issue within our church communities but one that poses a particularly thorny problem for society as a whole. That is why this book espouses views beyond the boundaries of the church. The reason is simply that, although the church is adequately representative of a lot that prevails in the Black community, it is not totally a representative location of societal ills. Yet I copiously refer to the church as it is my primary constituency.

Furthermore, domestic violence is an act of oppression and injustice. It is a social problem with dysfunctional violent patterns passed over many generations. In most cases, it is an unhealthy pattern of violent behaviors passed down from one generation to the next. Research studies have demonstrated that Christian couples and families also struggle with domestic violence. According to Dynna Castillo Portugal in the article "Faithful Pastoral Care: A Response to Domestic Violence Claiming the Right to Speak Up," many in church leadership, including some pastors, have failed to provide adequate pastoral care that victims desperately need due to misunderstandings, personal prejudices, assumptions, beliefs in traditional gender codes of behavior, and insufficient training and education on the issue of domestic violence. Authentic spiritual leaders, ministers, and pastoral care counselors are encouraged to remind victims that the power of Jesus Christ's death and resurrection is of real importance to them. Jesus came to break down the walls of dysfunctional partners, gender discrimination, and oppression. The Messiah of Israel came to confront the status quo, injustice, and societal corruption. Jesus came to bring reformation to old traditional belief systems. The Son of Man suffered for all of humanity, both male and female. Abused sisters must be encouraged because Jesus came to demonstrate that all women are valuable to the Heavenly Father. Females are created with worth and dignity, made in the image of God.

As a close to this introduction, I posit that pastoral care counselors and church leaders need to create a safe environment for all abused women, particularly women of color. Church leadership must ensure that abused women feel welcome to freely express themselves. Godly leaders should demonstrate a nonjudgmental attitude, genuine respect, boundless compassion, and unwavering emotional support. Additionally, they should provide critical material resources, make referrals to DV shelters, and even offer a safe haven whenever they encounter cases of domestic abuse.

Sonia Martin
Mount Vernon, New York,
United States of America
July 2024

CHAPTER 1

A Personal Connectedness

Couples counseling encourages the abuser to blame
the victim by examining her role in his problem. By
seeing the couple together, the therapist erroneously
suggests that the partner, too, is responsible for the
abuser's behavior. Many women have been beaten
brutally following couples counseling sessions in
which they disclosed violence or coercion. The
abuser alone must take responsibility for the assaults
and understand that family reunification is not his
treatment goal; the goal is to stop the violence.

—Linda G. Mills,
Violent Partners: A Breakthrough Plan
For Ending The Cycle of Abuse

One day, a few years ago, I received a rather distressing phone call. It was regarding a church member who had been murdered by her husband. Sally was a registered nurse who had met and fallen in love with a young man named Wayne in Jamaica, in the West Indies. Sally and Wayne had gotten married barely a year after they first met. Shortly thereafter, Wayne migrated to the United States and took up residence with Sally and her mother. As might be initially expected, Wayne had difficulty finding employment and soon became verbally and physically abusive of his wife.

Sally's mother insisted that Wayne be evicted from the house. Sally agreed with her mother and complied with the suggestion. A couple of weeks later, in a tragic twist to the entire episode, Sally's mother found her daughter lying prostrate on the living room floor. She had been stabbed to death.

Unfortunately, this is the common and sad ending to the narratives of many abused women who have experienced intimate partner violence. With each passing day, we continue to witness similar accounts of abused women like Sally, who are verbally, psychologically, and physically victimized and eventually murdered by their husbands or boyfriends.

It is no less disheartening that within many African American church congregations, we have many members of the clergy who learn of such incidences of domestic violence yet lack a wholesale understanding of what domestic violence actually means for victims. In the course of my extensive work in this field, I have discovered that many Black women in church congregations who find themselves in abusive relationships are taught to be submissive to their husbands, no matter how traumatic their domestic circumstances may be. Many such abused women actually believe that they have no right over their own bodies simply because they have been indoctrinated in the fatally flawed belief that their husbands are lords over them.

As might be expected, at the heart of the contention is the misinterpretation of certain Scriptures. For instance, Ephesians 5:22–23 (NIV) states, "Wives, submit to your husbands as to the Lord, for the husband is the head of his wife as Christ is the head of the church." Rather conveniently, these verses are misguidedly exploited and promoted by Bible teachers who ordinarily ought to know better and are used to enable abusive men.

Webster's Dictionary defines *submission* as "the condition of being submissive, humble, or compliant." Another definition of *submission* is the "act of submitting to the authority or control of another." By no sane implication does submission mean that a wife should become a punching bag for her husband. On the domestic front, submission means respecting your husband's point of view. It means humbly sharing your opinion with him. It means not invalidating him, especially in front of others. It means trusting his decision as a leader while feeling empowered to give your own point of view.

From the correct Christian perspective, a submissive wife is a supportive wife. She works together with her spouse and respects and supports him in their marriage. Within a Christian marriage, a wife freely expresses her thoughts, trusting her husband's response will lovingly support her and look out for her best interests. A Christian wife happily submits to her Christian husband because she knows every decision he makes will be done selflessly for her happiness and the good of their marriage.

However, when one looks at the issue of violence from a theological perspective, violence is a sin problem. Neena M. Malik and Kristin M. Lindahl are psychologists who focused their research on the dynamics of relationships. They found evidence to support the role of abuse of power in family violence. Power clearly plays a significant role in domestic violence. Psychologists believe that abuse of power is the root cause of domestic violence, although the research is still ongoing.

Steven R. Tracy, a professor of theology and ethics, writes, "Of all the social problems confronted by the church, domestic violence is surely one of the most misunderstood and mismanaged by church leaders." In Tracy's view, because of this lack of knowledge of the intricacies of family violence, there is a pervasive ineffectiveness in addressing the issue due to intransigence and cultural prohibition in even speaking about the topic, let alone addressing it headlong. Tracy explained that he had come to the knowledge that abusers misused their power to force and control women.

Study after study of victims of domestic violence who reached out to clergy for help revealed that these church leaders were of negligible help to those abused women. Tracy, who did extensive work on the subject, argued that too many pastors have often given misguided and harmful advice to abused women. The fact that many in ministry lack the education on how to offer adequate support to these hurting women, who are desperately seeking help, is a significant part of the problem. Domestic violence advocates continue to express the view that the church is failing to decisively confront the issue by enabling, concealing, and not properly managing reports of domestic violence. Sadly, if church leaders are not a part of the solution, they can only be qualified, unfortunately, as perpetuators of the problem.

It therefore becomes imperative for the leadership of the church to first acknowledge the problem of intimate partner violence and its negative effect on many Black church families. Next, the African American church leadership must sincerely evaluate its responsibility in addressing the issue of domestic violence by responding to a vital question: *will the Body of Christ take a stand in solidarity with oppressed women or with their abusers?* In this season, faith leaders need to be educated on the proper theological understanding of who God is and that God's heart is full of compassion for those who are oppressed.

Psalm 9:9 (NIV) says, "The Lord is a refuge for the oppressed, a stronghold in times of trouble." The only way church leaders can truly justify the huge responsibility they bear of shepherding their flock is by becoming true representatives of God's love and empathy for battered women.

I find that, on a personal note, I can experientially relate to the cultural undertones that explain many aspects of domestic violence. But first, permit me to once again refer to Elizabeth L. Gerhardt. She identified the fundamental motivations for the abuses directed toward females as an issue of cultural conditioning. In other words, culture plays a major role in violence against women. Culture influences the way human beings perceive things, behave, and communicate. Culture plays a significant role in influencing how we behave. In many respects, culture is like the blueprint that shapes how we think, act, and interact with others.

Culture can be defined as the principles, ideologies, and traditions carried over from one generation to another by a group of people. It is the way of life for a particular community. Being part of a culture creates a sense of belonging, which is the basis of most societies. An analogy that can help explain the influence of culture on behavior is to think of it as a set of instructions for a culinary recipe. Just like a recipe needs instructions to make a cake, culture provides instructions for how to behave in a particular society. It tells us what is considered acceptable behavior and what is not.

From a psychological point of view, culture influences our behavior in many ways. For example, the values and beliefs passed down from generation to generation can shape how we view the world and interact with people. We also learn about what is expected of our gender, age group, and social class from our culture. All of these can have an impact on our behavior. However, the influence of culture on behavior will vary depending on the society's specific cultural norms and values. To narrow down these influences to general behavioral tendencies or attributes of society would be difficult, mainly because cultures are as complex and multifaceted as they are unique and variable from region to region.

The place of my birth is uptown Kingston, also called Saint Andrew, in Jamaica, West Indies, which is one of the Caribbean islands, also called the West Indies. Jamaica is well-known for its gorgeous beaches and beautiful landscapes. That translates to being a product of a West Indian culture where the age-old patriarchal narrative, despite recent advances in gender equality and women's rights, remains a dominant feature of a society that has for long remained in the firm grip of male superiority that is misperceived at best and totally misguided at worst.

In my childhood years, corporal punishment was the norm in the home in which I was raised. I vividly recall multiple incidences of being subjected to verbal and emotional abuse. That unwholesome experience extended to the classroom setting, where there simply was no escaping the teacher's cudgel for any perceived infraction of rules that were more nebulous than specific. Worse, corporal punishment in the form of caning or whipping was applied to foster or encourage learning. The entire travesty would have been a laughable joke if it wasn't so patently ridiculous.

In the circumstances, one might think the church, the supposed holy bastion of all that is sane, normal, and moral in society, would be a refuge. Nothing could have been further from the unpleasant truth. The church offered a worse example of degradation. I can recall once, when I was sixteen years old, how I received a beating at church from my pastor. Suffice it to say that these experiences left a lasting negative impact on my emotional well-being.

It was not uncommon to regularly hear the now-too-familiar screams of a female next-door neighbor being physically assaulted by her husband. On a particularly harrowing day for her, the woman ran into my mother's house and asked my mother to hide her from her irate husband. What struck me as particularly odd was that, despite widespread awareness of the abuse this woman was regularly subjected to, no one in the sprawling community thought it fit to intervene in her plight, and so the physical assaults and beatings continued unabated. In many more ways than one, these childhood encounters with family violence would help program my subconscious for my own future experiences with intimate partner violence as an adult.

At the age of forty-three, I had my first experience with intimate partner violence. I suffered verbal, emotional, psychological, sexual, and physical assault at the hands of the man, an ordained pastor to whom I was married. It ought not to come as the least bit of surprise that the very idea of this book was birthed out of my personal journey and my horrendous experience as a victim of intimate partner violence. Yet I take consolation in the reassuring truth that this is also my own cathartic journey through the reclamation of my power and the healing of my traumatized psyche.

It is rather instructive that, prior to my personal experience with marital abuse, I had never had cause to even remotely consider the role church leadership or pastors play in domestic violence. My situation was rather peculiar. I was married to an ordained minister who had a master's degree in divinity and who was an associate pastor at a prominent Black church. This man, my ex-husband, was abusive to an uncommon extreme of savagery. To make matters infinitely worse, he was addicted to drugs and alcohol and on many occasions attempted to kill me with his bare hands, especially anytime he was inflamed by his insane jealousy.

Matters finally came to a head, and I had to be hospitalized because of attempted strangulation by my pastor husband. Upon discharge from the hospital, I sought assistance from the senior pastor of the church. The pastor met with both my ex-husband and myself at a joint meeting. Naturally, that was an extremely uncomfortable forum for me, since I was in mortal fear of relating the past multiple incidents of domestic violence. I felt ashamed to describe the seriousness and the severity of my terrible situation. During that couples' session, my ex-husband admitted to attempting to strangle me, yet minimized, if not denied, the frequency and severity of his abuse by falling on the dubious platitude, "This was due to a post-traumatic stress disorder episode. I didn't know what I was doing."

To my chagrin, the senior pastor never once held my ex-husband accountable, nor did he even broach the idea of a temporary separation or some plan to adequately address my safety. Instead, the pastor counseled me to continue to work on the marriage. In his words, "You made a vow to work on this marriage for better or for worse." I left the session with feelings of abject despair, utter helplessness, and total hopelessness. I returned home with a violent husband. The senior pastor's recommendation placed me in even greater danger, as it merely translated to being meekly acquiescent to whatever treatment my husband saw fit to subject me to. Naturally, I ended up in the hospital once again.

It is my belief that the senior pastor failed me because he lacked the insight to discern abuse and in his inability to respond appropriately. It was this traumatic experience that opened my eyes to the inadequate resources and unwise counseling that church leadership offers. I was saddened because I could have quite easily lost my life like countless women who remained in abusive relationships. Whichever way one views it, I was just one of a lucky few. All else is ineffectual commentary.

In the course of researching for this book, I spoke to quite a few Black women who have experienced domestic violence by an intimate partner and who remained in abusive relationships over a period of one or more years. The majority of these women were also attendees at a local African American church. Whether we can readily accept it or not, there are several major factors that bedevil every cultural denomination, and the Black church community is no exception. Such issues include gender inequality, faith contradictions, cultural anomalies, and economic hardship. All these issues impact the lives of women and their children. When the church neglects to address these issues, battered women are left with feelings of abandonment, rejection, and disempowerment. Domestic violence is horrific and unacceptable in every sense. Therefore, spiritual leadership in every tradition of faith can no longer remain in a state of denial of spousal abuse. Church administrators, pastors, and bishops must address, confront, and tackle the predicament of domestic violence.

My personal experience has accorded me the wisdom that, to unravel the complexities of intimate partner violence, we must engage in the exploration of emotions and thought processes, and we must conduct an examination of the meaning behind people's complex life experiences. We must also commit to systematically seeking answers to questions by examining various social situations and the individuals who inhabit those social settings. I realized rather quickly that, to obtain a better understanding of how to provide emotional support and offer resources and concrete services to abused women, it is important to give them the opportunity to verbalize their stories, the way I have related mine, and to allow them to gain a deeper perspective on the factors contributing to their unfortunate circumstances.

As with many abused women I spoke to, freely recalling and revealing some of my most painful and traumatic experiences actually provided me with insight and a greater understanding of those experiences. Such narratives can be used in educational research because of the connection between *history* and *learning*. I have also used the narratives of abused women to obtain a better understanding of the cycles of violence they were subjected to, the core components of their abusive situations, and the overall impact of their abusive encounters on their psychological well-being. This approach has allowed me to see how these women made any sense of their situation and how they subsequently relate with their families, communities, and culture.

As I discovered from my own experience, an abused woman craves empathy and a nonjudgmental disposition on the part of a counselor. It is a delicate assignment to get an abused woman to disclose what she has encountered, endured, and survived. This is principally due to an understandable fear of reprisal from her abusive intimate partner. Yet only frank and open discussions about her experiences can ultimately put her in a safe place. That safe place is as important as the totality of her life itself. For the abused woman, leaving an intimate partner violent relationship for a safe place can be critical yet vital to her emotional, psychological, and physical well-being.

CHAPTER 2

The Cultural Foundation of Abuse

In a verbally abusive relationship, the partner learns to tolerate abuse without realizing it, and to lose self-esteem without realizing it. She is blamed by the abuser and becomes the scapegoat. The partner is then the victim.

—Patricia Evans,
The Verbally Abusive Relationship: How to Recognize It, and How to Respond

consider it more than necessary to inaugurate the very vital contents of this book by first subjecting the sociocultural antecedents of abuse to exhaustive consideration. To acquit myself with more than passing credibility in that assignment, I will address certain key questions:

- What significant role does culture play in domestic violence?
- Using myself and my own narrative as a reference point, what are the contributions of my Jamaican culture to domestic abuse?
- What are the contributions of American culture to pervasive intimate partner abuse in American society?

- What teachings in the church have been used to enable and perpetuate the oppression of women?
- More specifically, how do the issues surrounding domestic violence relate to abused African American women in the church?

The word *culture* has many different meanings and connotes numerous interpretations. One of its definitions states, "Culture consists of customary beliefs, social forms, and material traits of a racial, religious, or particular group or society." Every individual, whether male or female, was conceived and went through gestational development in the womb of culture. Culture influences the way human beings perceive things, the way they behave, and the way they communicate. Culture drives a society's customs, beliefs, values, and traditions. An eminent psychologist describes culture as "the collective programming of the mind that distinguishes the members of one group or category of people from others."

Culture possesses the capacity to totally describe an individual's way of life. A society's culture can be expressed through traditions passed down from one generation to the next through writing, music, religion, family values, or learned behavior. Every individual learns to do things differently, principally based on the culture in which he or she was raised. Angelica-Nicoleta Neculaesei, an academic researcher at Alexandru Ioan Cuza University, Lasi, Romania, in her article "Culture and Gender Role Differences," states, "Culture influences human behavior; the social environment in which individuals are born and live shapes their attitudinal emotional reactions and perceptions." Therefore, within each society, male and female are treated according to the specific culture in which they were raised.

Within American society, culture is expressed in the beliefs, way of life, art, and customs shared and accepted by people in particular ways. Sociologists define *society* as people who interact in such a way as to share a common culture. The term *society* can also have a *geographic* meaning by referring to people who share a common culture in a particular location or territory. Society, therefore, describes a group of people who share a community, and a culture. By "community," sociologists refer to a definable region such as Brooklyn or Staten Island or Queens.

Within the United States, there are many subcultures, which are defined as "groups that share a specific identification, apart from a society's majority, even as the members exist within a larger society." Most certainly, America's subcultures evolved from the influx of immigrants from all over the world into America every year. In everyday conversations, people rarely distinguish between the terms *culture* and *society*, yet the terms have slightly different meanings that are important to a sociologist. To clarify matters, *a culture represents the beliefs and practices of a group, while society represents the people who share those beliefs and practices.* In a nutshell, neither society nor culture could exist without the other.

There is little doubt that individuals are most comfortable in the subculture to which they belong. Africans have endured a history of oppression and racism in American society. It is logical, therefore, to surmise that the culture of oppression and violence, whether in the home or the larger society, has been passed down from one generation to the next. Culture will, of compelling necessity, encompass the values and traditions that an individual learns from parents, teachers, pastors, and government officials. People necessarily become the products of what they learn, since learning, by itself, is a change in behavior resulting from experience. Russian physiologist Ivan Pavlov discovered *classical conditioning*, which is "a learning process that occurs through associations between an environmental stimulus and a naturally occurring stimulus." Pavlov, through his experiments, proved that all learning occurs through interactions with the environment, and the environment shapes behavior.

I grew up in the Jamaican culture, in which there was a preponderance of violence. Violence was a daily experience. In fact, a day in which one was not a witness to an act of violence could only be considered an oddity. The culture, all over the island of Jamaica, was strongly rooted in violence. Kingston, the capital city of the island, was particularly a bastion of violence, especially in the form of murders that were as irrational as they were senseless. In the era of my growth as a young girl in Jamaica, the prevailing culture totally embraced corporal punishment.

At home, I was subjected to verbal abuse, emotional abuse, and corporal punishment on an unrelenting daily basis. The roller coaster of punishment continued at school. As soon as you entered the classroom, there simply was no escaping the imminent prospect of being caned or flogged by the teacher for some misdemeanor or another. I am of a particularly fragile psychic sensitivity, because of which I hated, with uncommon passion, the day-to-day belittling, humiliation, and beatings that I received from my mother. Those verbal, emotional, and physical abuses would exert their lasting toll and their devastatingly negative impact on me.

I am the last of four children born to my mother and a father who died when I was only eighteen months of age. I grew up in a home with a single mother, grandmother, my uncle, and my three siblings. Whenever I fell short of her rigid expectations and infringed on any of her unbearably exacting standards, my mother would physically beat me across my back with a belt. When my mother was at work, my uncle would take over from where my mother stopped. He would physically beat my hands with a cane whenever I was perceived as being disrespectful to him.

But what I considered most devastating and by far most damaging was my mother's verbal tirades against me. Indeed, to inflict a physical beating on me was one matter. To subject me to unspeakable verbal humiliation was quite another. One day, my mother gleefully and callously informed me that she considered me the ugliest of her four children. It was routine for her to say things like, "You are stupid," and "You will never amount to anything without me." On the sidelines of my ordeal at the hands of my own mother was the terror that was my oldest brother, who was about ten years older than my younger brother. My older brother was taller and bigger than my younger brother, and he would regularly beat up his younger brother to the point where I often had nightmares of my older brother killing my younger brother.

Yet I believe that my mother was merely a product of the culture of her native Jamaica. She knew no better. She was raised in a

Christian home in which she was the eldest of eight children and in an environment in which she was told children were to be seen and not heard. Her parents were members of the Seventh Day Baptist Church, where her father was an elder. He was also a strict disciplinarian. By the natural extension of upbringing, my mother also emerged as a strict disciplinarian. My mother would often tell her children of the many beatings that her father gave her and made it an unwavering point of duty to show us scarified evidence of those beatings on her legs. I grew up thinking that my grandfather was an uncommonly cruel man. Yet even he was a mere product of the culture in which he was raised.

As I grew into adulthood, I began to totally reject this culture of corporal punishment, especially because it was not only children who were at the receiving end of beatings in Jamaican society. The culture also encouraged the severe, daily beating of women by their husbands. Those violent tendencies were passed down from the days of slavery when slaves were flogged mercilessly whenever they disobeyed the slave masters. So we had come full circle. We had a multicausal and multigenerational pattern that was based on the economic and political power structures of slavery.

To further entrench my psyche in the vicious cycle, as I grew up, I became regularly exposed to domestic violence. Suffice it to say that domestic violence is one of the worst and most pervasive of the negative cultural norms of Jamaican society. Women were frequently physically beaten by their husbands, while the government and law enforcement conveniently looked the other way. I easily recall my first exposure to domestic violence. I was only ten years old. I heard a woman screaming as she was being physically beaten by her husband. The woman lived next door to my mother's house. She ran into our house, pleading with my mother to hide her. The beating went on for many more years, and no one in that small community ever intervened. Within Jamaican society, this sort of violence was an acceptable way of life. It was simply the norm.

Deeply rooted feelings of fear, guilt, shame, sleep disturbances, sadness, and depression are natural accompaniments of exposure to domestic violence. In retrospect, with regard to my past abusive relationship, I have arrived at the realization that my childhood exposure to domestic violence had a profound, long-lasting impact on me. As a child, I was exposed to both corporal punishment in the home and at school, and this had a lasting negative impact on me. Many children grow up thinking that this learned behavior is perfectly normal. Yet what we have here is merely a consequence of early classical conditioning, which is learned behavior that occurs through associations between an environmental stimulus and a naturally occurring stimulus. Violence is learned through interactions and by observing the environment, and this shapes behaviors into good or bad.

According to the World Health Organization (WHO), "Cultural and social norms are highly influential in shaping individual behavior, including the use of violence. Cultural norms can protect against violence, and also support and encourage the use of it." Cultural acceptance of violence, either as a normal method of resolving conflict or as a usual part of rearing a child, is a risk factor for all types of interpersonal violence because people do what has been done to them. Hurt people then go on to hurt others, and breaking the pattern necessarily becomes an act of conscious decision.

It is an incontrovertible fact that in certain parts of the world, female children are valued less in society than males. In such climes, female children are considered to have less social and economic potential than male children. In some cultures, physical violence is an acceptable way to resolve conflicts within a relationship. In many parts of the world, also, a man has a right to assert power over a woman since he is considered socially superior. Even though there was a persecutor/victim relationship in slavery, it easily became the model for the male/female relationship among the victims.

My childhood exposure to domestic violence was a contributing factor to my own experience in an abusive relationship with my abusive ex-husband. It is my strong belief that both corporal punishment and domestic violence are lasting effects of slavery, where slaves were flogged and many slaves were lynched and castrated when they disobeyed the slave masters.

From a strictly cultural perspective, Jewish culture in the first century was decidedly patriarchal. Women were responsible for bearing the children, rearing them, and maintaining a hospitable home. It was considered taboo for men to greet women in public. Some Jewish writers of Jesus's era, such as Philo Judaeus, taught that women should never leave the home except to go to the synagogue. Young women were almost always under the protection and authority of a man—her father or her husband—and more often than not, women married rather early. At the Temple in Jerusalem, women were restricted to an outer court. In synagogues, they were separated from the men and not permitted to read aloud. In the area of religious practice, women were in many ways overlooked.

Against this extensive early background of cultural subjugation, I entertain little doubt in my mind as to the powerful role that church culture plays in shaping a woman's experience of domestic violence. All my life, I have registered a physical presence at church, sometimes four times a week. I grew up in the Seventh Day Baptist Church of God and was conditioned to believe that wives should be submissive to their husbands. I grew up believing that men are the heads of women, meaning that men are superior to women. We can easily predict what happens when a woman thinks like I did—that her husband is her lord and master. This sort of mindset only sets the stage for women to accept the bondage of domestic violence.

Understanding cultural perspectives on domestic violence means learning about the specific attitudes toward domestic violence within a victim's culture and within the legal system of that victim's home country. Many Christian women of color in abusive relationships are of the opinion that they were taught in church to be submissive to their husbands and to do so out of duty. Many of these women believe that they have no right over their own bodies because their husbands are lords over them. This is often the misconception promoted by advice from clergy, ministers, or other members of the church. We might argue that many men in the church may feel that failure to lord it over their partners might easily translate to failing in one of God's injunctions to them in their position as master and lord of the household.

Abused Black women in the church may feel worthless and powerless. Throughout the cycles of domestic violence, the victim's ego has been literally dismantled, leaving her with feelings of disempowerment, helplessness, and powerlessness. As a result, many domestic violence advocates are of the opinion that the best way to help survivors is to give them back control of their lives. Let's face it. The double jeopardy of *racism* and *sexism* in American society leaves women of color at a position of dismal disadvantage. This makes the model of empowerment one of the most effective goals of intervention where they are concerned. Empowerment occurs when there is a conscious internal shift, and the abused church woman begins to understand that she is worthy of respect and love. Empowerment means an abused woman is taking back her power. This enablement allows abused Black women to acquire an increased sense of personal control over their lives, such that they can begin to feel good about themselves.

CHAPTER 3

The Psychology of Abuse

Abuse is a control tactic. Its aim is to
break you and make you submit.

—M. Wakefield,
Are You in an Emotionally Abusive Relationship?

American culture is fundamentally rooted in power. That culture has been advanced to one of control and the misuse of power. Psychologists define power as "an individual's relative capacity to modify others' states by providing or withholding resources or administering punishments." While these resources can be both material and social, in the average concept and interpretation of power, the capacity to influence others is what occupies the position of primary importance. This type of power is termed *social power* because it is derived from one's relationship to others. Psychologists believe that *power* and *control* are essentially at the root of domestic violence. This is the classic *misuse of power* that is seen when people allow power to get to their heads and employ that power for self-gratification. Many abusive individuals, mostly men, use controlling behavior and coercive control to obtain and maintain control over their victims.

Sociologists Johannes Weiss and Thomas Schwietring report that there is sufficient evidence to suggest that power and control are fundamentally the root cause of domestic violence. "Power appears to be the root cause of all evil in human societies." Therefore, by using manipulative tactics such as threats, beatings, and psychological fear, the male abuser subjects the abused female to the psychological, physical, sexual, or financial bondage of abuse. I personally see the entire issue primarily from the perspective of the abuse of power, and that perspective addresses men like Emperor Nero of the Roman Empire, who imposed impossible taxes on the people, tortured many people to death, and burned many Christians alive, and some of the early followers of Jesus Christ to lions. History tells us of Adolf Hitler, who at the peak of his power killed over six million Jews in what is known today as the Holocaust.

Male usage of power and domination was first associated with a patriarchal society in which males controlled the levers of power and dominated females. The history of American society clearly establishes the misuse of power and the oppression of the Indians. Slavery will have to count as one of the greatest human monuments to the abuse of power in the form of combined oppression, domination, and subjugation. All the major European powers were involved in slavery, but by the early eighteenth century, Britain became the world's leading slave-trading power. The slavers, men of tremendous power, totally exploited Africa by robbing the African people of their wealth and identity and then bringing them to America in chains.

For decades, women have been the unwitting and unwilling brunt of male oppression. Women's rights activists, researchers, and programmers have emphasized how patriarchal systems shape social expectations, in both functional and ideological terms, to maintain male superiority over women. According to Weiss and Schwietring, "When 'power' is spoken of, the first association is that of the power of man over man, of power as suppression of the free will by 'commands' and 'obedience.' 'Power' can easily appear in this connection as the root of all evil in human societies and as the opposite of freedom as such." The argument can be made that a great deal of domestic violence was birthed out of the cruelties of slavery, coupled with the behavior learned from an environment of violence. Misuse of power, controlling behavior, and coercive control are the ways by which an abusive individual obtains and maintains power and control over another person, in order to subject that person to psychological, physical, sexual, or financial abuse.

Power and its misuse are great contributors to the phenomenon of domestic violence. Neena Malik and Kristin Lindahl, and other workers in the fields of psychology, mental health, and social work, have long discovered in the past few decades that domestic violence is on the increase. Malik and Lindahl, in particular, found that there are several disagreements concerning the contributing factors of violence between intimate partners. To streamline their work, they focused their research on the dynamics of relationships and the crucial role of power. I am inclined to agree with them that *abuse of power* plays a major role in domestic violence. Males, by their biological makeup, are bigger, stronger, and more aggressive than females. American men, more often than not, possess greater financial power than women, as their pay rates tend to be higher. Tapping into my own experience, my former husband was 6 feet, 5 inches, compared to my height of 5 feet, 7 inches, and he made significantly more money than I did.

Furthermore, Malik and Lindahl stated that overall, contemporary literature supports the fact that power plays a fundamental role, or is one of the root causes of domestic violence. Controlling abusers use various tactics to exercise power and control over their victims. Those tactics themselves are mainly psychologically abusive, but sometimes are physical. Control may be asserted through economic abuse, thereby limiting the victim's actions as they may then lack the necessary resources to resist the abuse. The goal of the abuser is to control and intimidate the victim or to influence them to feel that they do not have an equal voice in the relationship. Emotional abuse is any type of abuse that is emotional rather than physical in nature. It can include anything from verbal abuse and constant criticism to more subtle tactics, such as intimidation and manipulation.

Dr. Tricia Bent-Goodley is a professor of social work and director of the doctoral program at Howard University's School of Social Work. According to her, even though there has been a tremendous volume of experimental research gathered over the past 20 years on African Americans and domestic violence, there are still many unanswered questions. She says these studies tell us that over 1.5 million women nationwide seek medical treatment for injuries related to abuse each year. Her unequivocal conclusion is that domestic violence significantly undermines healthy African American families and communities.

It is true that domestic violence poses serious mental and physical health risks to African American women. African American women, like all other women who are abused, may experience mental health issues, such as anxiety attacks, post-traumatic stress disorder (PTSD), depression, acute stress disorder, and suicidal ideations and attempts. These women suffer physical consequences of abuse, such as rape, unwanted pregnancies, hypertension, increased substance abuse, suicide attempts, and homicide. Domestic violence is the leading cause of injuries to women between the ages of fifteen and forty-four and is more common than robberies, automobile accidents, and cancer deaths combined. The general health considerations are staggering and even more alarming for African Americans, resulting in one out of four women dying each year. Tricia Bent-Goodley concludes that although domestic violence cuts across race, socioeconomic status, education, and income distinctions, it has been estimated that African Americans experience a disproportionate amount of domestic violence compared with white Americans. African American women are more likely to kill a partner and are at the same time twice as likely as white women to be killed because of domestic violence.

As we take a closer look at abused church women of color, we discover that many psychological factors come into play. In general, many of these psychological factors also have an enormous negative impact on many abused married women between the ages of twenty-five and thirty-five within the Black church communities. These psychological factors include, but are not limited to, childhood trauma, low self-worth, and the vicious cycle of entrapment by what I call the *fire of fear*; isolation from family and friends, and a feeling of confusion. Additionally, there are other psychological stressors such as financial dependence on the abuser, the lack of a college education, unemployment, and disadvantaged economic status. These psychological issues, more often than not, greatly contribute to an abused woman's feeling of *helplessness* and *hopelessness.* Most abused women in the African American church struggle with low self-esteem. In many cases, self-esteem and domestic violence go hand in hand. Low self-esteem can arise from a variety of factors and can be a serious issue for women who are victims of domestic violence.

It is logical to assume that an abused woman with low self-esteem is likely to remain in an abusive relationship. This can lead to serious injuries and even death. Still, a healthy self-esteem alone cannot combat domestic violence, since even a woman with high self-esteem can be affected by domestic violence. Be that as it may, I feel that the woman with a better self-image will be more empowered to leave an abusive relationship, and that is what is more important to focus on. Women with low self-esteem feel that they cannot do better than the situation in which they find themselves, and this sense of defeat makes them far less likely to leave than a woman who has high self-esteem and can stand up for herself. According to Toni Collinson, "In many cases, self-esteem and domestic violence go hand in hand. Low self-esteem can be brought on by a variety of factors." Most offenders, Collinson writes, tend to prey on women who have low self-esteem, realizing that the victim will want and need them no matter what they do. It is, therefore, essential that children are loved and accepted by their parents. When parents don't love and accept each child as a special human being, then individuals cannot develop healthy self-worth.

Additionally, the average abused Black church woman will not leave her abusive marriage because she feels trapped in it. Many of these women are confused and fearful of going out on their own, while some stay because of their children. The feeling of confusion is primarily compounded by the fear that they cannot survive without their batterer. Fear is one of the major factors in domestic violence and is one of the main reasons why many women remain in abusive relationships. Many abused Black church women live with verbal threats of physical harm by their abusive church husbands.

I invite you to imagine the sheer terror an abused woman experiences when a gun is pointed at her head. What does a punch in the face do to a woman's mind? I recall my former husband, an abusive pastor, taking off all of my clothes and threatening to push me out the front door on an extremely cold winter night. These are some of the abuses that cause the fear that entraps abused women.

According to psychologists, children learn behaviors, good or bad, from the environment they grow up in. Based on my own experience of domestic violence and from working through my issues in therapy, I believe that domestic violence often begins in our original homes. If a girl has been verbally abused, as I was on an ongoing basis, and she is constantly belittled and told that she will never amount to anything, that girl will internalize all the damaging words and begin to believe that she has no worth. That girl believes on an unconscious level that she has no value. Similarly, if a girl has been subjected to corporal punishment and is flogged on a daily basis, she begins to learn that this is normal behavior. Women like me who tend to attract abusive partners have been preconditioned for violence of some type or another during their childhood.

Dr. Carolyn West, a domestic violence expert, found that "many African American women are at elevated risk for nonfatal and lethal intimate partner violence" during research conducted to review these women's current knowledge, with a focus on the sociodemographic factors that make this population particularly vulnerable to abuse. Trauma victims are haunted by memories that feel completely real and can cause the victims to become silent sufferers who believe that their lives are destined to repeat past events. Experiences in a person's life can trigger a recurring experience of the original trauma, which makes healing from the original trauma an extremely important goal.

Many abused women of color, like most abused women, will encounter some form of isolation from their family of origin. Incredibly, isolation of the abused woman is one of the tools that an abuser employs to control her. An abuser will often check his victim's cellphone to see if any members of her family or friends call her. He may go as far as to threaten to kill her dog. By using these tactics, men who abuse their wives keep these women isolated and alone so that they can continue to abuse them.

Countless abused Black church women remain in abusive marriages or relationships because of financial dependence on their abusive husbands or boyfriends. This is due to several contributing factors, such as poverty, lack of college education, and unemployment. Even when victims of domestic abuse do leave their partners, ruined credit scores, inconsistent employment histories, legal issues, or chronic debt threaten their future financial security, and this compels many of them to return to their abusers. Many people don't understand why women who have left abusive relationships very often return to the same relationships. Many people, in blaming these abused Black women for returning, even suggest that the victim might possibly enjoy being abused. The rationalization is, "If they didn't like being abused, they would leave and not return, right?" Yet the reasons why abused Black women return to abusive relationships can be extremely complex.

Kerri Ann Renzulli, a personal finance journalist based in London, writes that some of these women have limited options because those who leave often face one or more additional barriers, the major one being a lack of money. Many abused women who are unemployed have at least one dependent child, possess no property, and lack access to cash or bank and credit accounts. A lack of money is a major contributing factor and the reason why a significant proportion of women return to an abusive relationship. Many of these women are unable to manage on their own due to a lack of finances. Equally incredible is the research finding that *economic dependency in women* and *emotional dependency in men* independently contribute to domestic partner abuse risk and that high levels of emotional dependency in an abused partner may reduce the likelihood that the victimized person will terminate the relationship.

CHAPTER 4

The Misguided Case for Male Dominance

> Growing up as a boy, we were taught that men had
> to be tough, had to be strong, had to be courageous,
> dominating—no pain, no emotions, with the exception
> of anger—and definitely no fear—that men are in
> charge, which means women are not; that men lead, and
> you should just follow and do what we say; that men
> are superior, women are inferior; that men are strong,
> women are weak; that women are of less value—property
> of men—and objects, particularly sexual objects.
> —Tony Porter in a 2010 TED Talk Show that
> *GQ Magazine* hailed as one of the "Top 10
> TED Talks Every Man Should See"

From a purely theological perspective, the concept of male dominance has long been rooted in Hebrew Scripture, where the paternal blessing was traditionally bestowed on the eldest son. Carolyn Custis James, a popular speaker for women's conferences and Christian organizations and the author of *Malestrom: Manhood Swept into the Currents of a Changing World*, articulated the belief that "male authority over women has become a hallmark of patriarchy. Indeed, that is precisely the meaning of patriarchy."

The patriarchs were males who possessed wealth, owned land and slaves, and held power. It is this issue of patriarchy that is at the center of domestic violence, where men view women as their property. This has created the ongoing universal dilemma in which women are oppressed, and the results have impacted the Christian community in no small measure.

The plan of the Creator, however, was for males and females to live in loving partnership within the family unit, not to exist in a state of dysfunction. "So God created man in His own image; in the image of God He created him; male and female He created them. Then God blessed them, and God said to them, 'Be fruitful and multiply; fill the earth and subdue it; have dominion over the fish of the sea, over the birds of the air, and over every living thing that moves on the earth'" (Genesis 1:27–28). Love is one of the predominant themes in Scripture, and its teachings are well documented in modern theology. There are many Scripture passages to support the argument that violence is not encouraged, such as, "'Beloved, do not avenge yourselves… Vengeance is Mine, I will repay,' says the Lord" (Romans 12:19), and, "Love your neighbor as yourself" (Matthew 22:39).

James Newton Poling, professor of pastoral care, counseling, and theology at Garrett-Evangelical Theological Seminary, is a trained pastoral psychotherapist who has worked for many years with male abusers. He is a well-known expert on the topic of male violence. He wrote, "Images of God in the New Testament condemn human violence forcefully." However, despite copious biblical evidence reinforcing love, many Christian spouses continue to indulge in violence.

There has been extensive research on the ideology of male dominance. Clinical psychologists Neena Malik and Kristin Lindahl, whom I quoted copiously in the previous chapter, paid special attention in their research to the changing aspects of relationships and the vital role of the misuse of power. They found substantial evidence that abuse of power plays a significant role in family violence. This evidence suggests a correlation between the misuse of power and domestic maltreatment. Psychologists believe that abuse of power is the root cause of domestic violence.

Feminists Silvia McGill Straka and Lyse Montminy explored some theoretical perspectives through the lens of the mismanagement of power and control. Common themes that emerged from their study were "the complexity of the power dynamics, patterns of abuse, verbal condescending, and the role of fear in psychological abuse." Male dominance, the cycle of abuse, and suggestions for seeking help for safety were made to differentiate between *abuse* with power dynamics and *mistreatment* and to evaluate the role of aggressor pathologies. In this deadly entrapment, Straka and Montminy explain, "The abuse of power and control is usually played by the abuser using different tactics to dominate, and the victim submitting to it out of a fear of being rejected and unloved."

A countless number of female victims of intimate partner violence relationships have experienced verbal intimidation, emotional condescension, and physical assaults. Consequently, many of these women suffer from physical as well as psychological trauma, with damaging and long-lasting health outcomes. The Centers for Disease Control (CDC) reports, "Four million women per year are victims of violence perpetrated, in many cases, by men who vowed to love, honor, and cherish them. Approximately 1,200 women will be killed every year by those same men." Many women suffer from short-term and long-lasting emotional, physical, and financial consequences. Females who have been victimized by intimate partners find themselves vulnerable to developing psychological fear, PTSD, insomnia, anxiety, depressed mood, substance use and abuse illness, and many other serious physical health issues. Additionally, statistics demonstrate, "Black women are three times more likely to be killed by a current or former partner than members of other racial groups."

Authors Catherine Itzin, Ann Taket, and Sarah Barter-Godfrey explain, "Domestic violence can take place in any intimate relationship, and the great majority of it is perpetrated by men against women."

According to Tjaden and Thoennes, research on violence against women has exploded in the past twenty-five years, particularly in the areas of intimate family violence and sexual assault. In spite of this plethora of research, there are still many gaps that exist in our understanding of domestic violence executed against Black women. The work conducted by Tjaden and Thoennes clearly outlines the percentage, numbers, and demographics of ethnic groups who have suffered in intimate partner relationships. There is insufficient reliable supporting evidence on minority women's experiences with domestic violence, such as the frequency of incidents, but less information about abused women and the correlation between childhood trauma, successive oppression, and persecution. To further drive home the point, Kroeger and Nagon-Clark write, "Another danger to which victims of abuse are peculiarly susceptible is that of suicide. Thirty-five to 40 percent of abused women attempt suicide. Wife abuse accounts for 25 percent of suicides by all US women and 50 percent of suicides by African American women." All the experiences from intimate partner relationships are psychologically traumatic and emotionally demeaning, resulting in many abused women suffering from depressed moods. In my personal experience, the consequences of domestic violence were psychologically painful. I suffered from a constant feeling of tremendous fear, shame, and self-blame. I also experienced nightmares, a gloomy disposition, flashbacks, depression, and hypervigilance. My verdict is simply that the misplaced and misguided concept of male dominance has done incalculable harm to society.

The church community bears a heavy burden of guilt. According to Catherine Clark Kroeger and James R. Beck in their groundbreaking book *Women, Abuse, and the Bible: How Scripture Can Be Used to Hurt or Heal,* some in the church community, in an attempt to minimize and justify violence against women, have misinterpreted the Holy Scriptures. They gave examples of Augustine, one of the early church fathers, who argued that women were inferior to men. Augustine's theology proposes that males are the head, and females should be in submission to their husbands. According to Kroeger and Beck, Augustine held the view that "one woman's lack of submission to her husband led him to commit adultery." Many pastors continue to teach and encourage abused Christian women to stay and be submissive to their husbands. This is based on the view that God created man first and that woman was created after man. The authors state, "I find it difficult to understand this in any other way than as an assertion of male headship and female submission that is based on the view that God created women in such a way that they are gullible." I totally disagree that man is superior simply because he was created first. God made man and woman to be in partnership, where both are chief executives in the management of the affairs of the Earth.

Kroeger and Beck further write on the term *kephale*, which traditionally means "authority over," and *authentein*, which is translated in the Bible as "to have authority over," and the interpretation of Genesis 1–3 of the relationship between the man and the woman, the biblical examples of women in positions of leadership, and the meaning of submission and silence for women. They admit that there has always been a great debate in the church about the headship of men and that the supporting arguments for male headship have been used to oppress women in the church, in the home, and in the community. In 1 Corinthians 11:3, Paul writes, "I would have you know that the head of every man is Christ; and the head of the woman is the man; and the head of Christ is God." Paul goes on to say in Ephesians 5, "Wives, submit yourselves unto your own husbands, as unto the Lord. For the husband is the head of the wife, even as Christ is the head of the church: and he is the savior of the body. Therefore, as the church is subject unto Christ, so let the wives be to their husbands in everything" (Ephesians 5:22–24).

In my personal experience, most Bible teachers and pastors have almost always emphasized the importance of the woman submitting to her husband, not quite as Paul states in Ephesians 5:21, "Submitting yourselves one to another in the fear of God." Therein lies the crucial difference. Therein lies the convenient variance between Paul's teaching and the convenient interpretation of today's pastor, purely to suit his own purpose. There needs to be wholesome teaching and interpretation of the Scriptures so that husbands and wives are encouraged to treat each other with respect and dignity.

Tony Porter is the CEO of A Call to Men. He is an author, educator, and activist working to advance gender and racial justice and create a more equitable society. Porter is internationally recognized for his efforts to prevent violence against women while promoting healthy, respectful manhood. He is a leading voice on issues of manhood, male socialization, and preventing violence against all women and girls. He is the author of the globally acclaimed book *Stepping Out of the Man Box*. In a recent TED Talk, he discusses what it means for men, women, sons, and daughters when the social pressure of masculinity confines men. To quote him, "Growing up as a boy, we were taught that men had to be tough, had to be strong, had to be courageous, dominating—no pain, no emotions, with the exception of anger—and definitely no fear—that men are in charge, which means women are not; that men lead, and you should just follow and do what we say; that men are superior, women are inferior; that men are strong, women are weak; that women are of less value—property of men—and objects, particularly sexual objects."

Porter gives these common socializations the moniker the Man Box, which contains all the stereotypical, hypermasculinized ways in which men are expected to behave and how those same expectations say volumes about how little our society values women and femininity. In that talk, Porter shares a personal discussion he had with a young athlete about how it would hypothetically feel if his football coach compared his playing skill to that of a girl in front of his teammates. The athlete responded, "It would destroy me." Porter draws a clear conclusion: if being compared to a girl would destroy this young man, what does it say about how our society views women's worth? He posits that it is time for men to look inside themselves to understand how their male privilege impacts how they value the women in their lives. Men need to peer inside Porter's Man Box and start to deconstruct the trappings of masculinity and the role it plays in women's equity.

To express matters clearly, Tony Porter addresses the issue of the collective socialization of men, which he also calls the Man Box, defining it as the societal conditioning, beginning in homes, where boys are taught what it means to be a man. Boys are programmed by the school of societies that set the expectations of what it means to be men. Boys are taught that boys don't cry because showing emotions demonstrates internal weakness and fear. Boys learn, most often, from the men in their lives. Many men learned to be aggressive and to demonstrate power and control over women. Little boys, from the time of their birth, are taught certain expectations. Boys are told that they are physically stronger than girls. Yes, boys are all but placed in a *man box* by their parents, teachers, church leaders, the community, and the society in which they live.

Furthermore, this socialization of men is deeply rooted in the culture of patriarchy that is still dominant in most parts of the world. As I already mentioned, Carolyn Custis James, in her book *Malestrom: Manhood Swept into the Currents of a Changing World*, explains, "Male authority over women becomes a hallmark of patriarchy… Indeed, that is precisely the meaning of patriarchy." Patriarchal traditions are rooted in Hebrew Scripture, where generational wealth was passed to the firstborn son. In many cultures all over the world, patriarchy still retains pervasive relevance because only the first-born son can inherit his parents' entire estate. In addition, Custis James states, "Historically, men have held a monopoly on positions of power and leadership in the world." One only needs to examine the concept of male power to understand why, for many years, power has been the exclusive preserve of white males in America. Men are still in positions of power in governments and most organizations as presidents, CEOs, and members of executive boards. Even in the church, women continue to be discriminated against and restricted to certain roles.

However, in the book *Malestrom*, Carolyn Custis James expresses the view that males and females are inseparable. So if there is a Man Box, then there is also a Woman Box. Society has also placed girls and boys in boxes from which some never escape. The author explained that gender roles are defined by culture, and society sets the expectations of what it means to be a male or a female. Girls are taught in church that they are the weaker sex; girls are told that there are lower standards for them and that expectations established by various cultures have been designed for them in particular. Girls are told that they are born to be caretakers, but many girls are not taught how to take care of themselves. Girls are told that when they grow up, they can only have certain professions, such as housewives, teachers, and nurses.

On the other hand, Tony Porter articulates that in our society, "Men are strong, women are weak; men are superior, women are inferior; men view women as property, of less value than men, objects, and especially sex objects." This concept of men viewing women as mere objects only helps to desensitize, minimize, and contribute to the attitude toward violence against women. Is there a relationship between how boys were culturally oriented and the proliferation of violence against women? Absolutely, yes. If a boy was taught that girls are of less value than him, then he would treat girls with disrespect. This boy was not taught how to value girls, so when he grows up, he only knows how to abuse or misuse women. Dr. Elizabeth Gerhardt writes, "Violence against women and girls is a human rights problem that impacts the lives of millions of families and communities." I concur with Dr. Gerhardt that violence against women and girls is a human rights issue that needs to be addressed by both men and women. In addition, Dr. Mary Ellsberg, in her presentation in the video "Ending Violence Against Women," says, "Around the world, 1 in 3 women will be beaten or raped by an intimate partner in her lifetime. That is over 700 million women." Dr. Ellsberg reported from her studies, "Numbers matter but faces equally matter." She spoke about the stories of women who are daily beaten, and who live in fear for their lives and the lives of their children. According to the World Health Organization (WHO), "Violence against women is the number one health concern for women." Many health conditions result from domestic violence, such as heart problems, anxiety, and depression. Many women are sexually assaulted, and others are murdered.

Most often, patterns and cultural tendencies are passed down from one generation to the next. They are also passed down to our sons and daughters through learned behaviors from their environment. In essence, children live what they learn. Men and women were placed in a box; these are called cultural norms. However, it is important to note that after the fall of man, both males and females were placed in one box, a condition called *sin*. Scripture states, "All have sinned and come short of the glory of God" (Romans 3:23). We all need the Savior. That is the reason the Savior came. As Jesus proclaimed, "The Spirit of the LORD is upon Me Because He has anointed Me To preach the gospel to the poor; He has sent Me to heal the brokenhearted, To proclaim liberty to the captives And recovery of sight to the blind, To set at liberty those who are oppressed" (Luke 4:18). Jesus came to set us free from all forms of oppression. He came to set men free from the Man Box and women free from the Woman Box. He came to liberate men and women from the chains that have bound them to the culture of oppression. John 8:36 says, "So if the Son sets you free, you will be free indeed." He came to set us free from sin. I am so grateful for the good news of salvation, for He came to set me free.

I spent many years in a church that encouraged women to submit to their husbands. This theological view resulted in abusive tendencies inherited from past generations, which were fostered for a time in my marriage. I struggled with feelings of disempowerment, failing to express my views and opinions due to fear of retaliation from my ex-husband. I entered a vicious and unhealthy cycle until I attended a fundraiser for abused women.

As the speaker described some of the controlling and domineering behaviors of the typical predator, my husband instantly experienced the conviction that he was exercising power over me, as opposed to treating me as an equal partner. That encounter placed us on a path of healing and recovery. I am amazed at how much a poor understanding of the Scriptures actually fueled those unhealthy power dynamics in our relationship. The theology of submission and the misinterpretation of Scripture continue to be promoted in many churches by pastors and those in church leadership.

There are still Bible teachers who quote the Scriptures when they counsel abused women, telling many women, as I was told by my pastor, "God hates divorce, so stay and work out the problem, because you made a vow for better or for worse." Many pastors counsel women in the presence of their abusive husbands. This is a dangerous practice that needs to be terminated because it places the lives of abused women in even more danger. Yet I thank God for a particular pastor whom I confided in, telling him how many times my abusive former husband had tried to strangle me. This pastor looked me in the eyes and said, "Sonia, you need to run for your life." I am extremely grateful to God that I survived to tell my story.

CHAPTER 5

Theology of Freedom
and the Imago Dei

That is, the imago Dei offered the foundational
human identity which is deeper than any socially-
constructed identities, such as racial identities.
—Hak Joon Lee, "Martin Luther King Jr., Archbishop
Desmond Tutu, and the Quest for Justice and
Reconciliation," *The Journal of Social Encounters*, 2022

ntimate partner violence has a direct and major impact on the identity, ego, self-worth, and dignity of abused women of color. Most male perpetrators use tactics of social isolation, fear, verbal belittling, and coercive controlling behaviors, creating feelings of entrapment and low self-esteem in abused women. Many abused Black Christian women who attend church turn to the Scriptures for answers to their internal conflicts as they relate to their individuality and uniqueness as human beings.

According to the Genesis records of creation, God created humanity in His image (Genesis 1:27 NRSV). Drawing from the creation story, one of the questions this book takes under consideration is, what is the true meaning of males and females being fashioned in the image of God? Through the biblical teaching of the image of God, the Scriptures confirm the value, dignity, and worth

34

of all people regardless of cultural background, gender, education, class, or financial status.

From a theological perspective, the Genesis record provides biblical scholars with a better understanding of the meaning of humanity being created in the image of God. If Scripture is to be believed, are males and females created equally in the image of God? The Genesis record offers scholars, church leaders, persons of faith, and people of other religions a unique perspective on biological sex and prevailing conceptions of gender. Male and female were created to equally enjoy their inheritance, birthright of freedom, and to be sovereign lords of the earth, not over each other.

Scripture's Teaching on Biological Sex and Gender

(1) Scripture confirms that male and female are created in the image of God. Genesis 1:26–27 reads, "Then God said, 'Let us make man in our image, after our likeness…' So God created man in his own image, in the image of God he created him; male and female he created them."

Genesis 1:26–27 clarifies that the Hebrew term "Adam" refers to the generic species of humanity composed of men and women. There is no uncertainty in support of biblical scholars on this interpretation. Genesis 5:2–3 affirms and provides the following definition: "When God created humankind, he made him in the likeness of God. Male and female, he created them, and he blessed them and named them humankind when they were created." Therefore, the "image of God in man and woman" offers accessible knowledge to surpass the issue of the masculine and feminine descriptions.

For God the Creator, who demonstrates his sovereignty in the holy Scriptures, transforms ancient identities and societal establishments in acknowledgment of the Eternal One. What has emerged is that whatever one's personal interpretation or understanding of the meaning of *image* and *likeness* of God, individuals must identify and acknowledge that the sacred text unequivocally establishes that humanity's depiction, likeness, and appearance are similar to the Creator God. Humanity, both male and female, were created to partake equally in having dominion over the earth, the plants, fishes, and animals. Men and women share a mutual human self-possession and dignity.

(2) An appropriate view of the image of God affirms that humans, both male and female, were created with different biological and functional characteristics, which include hormones, reproductive organs, and chromosomes. There is no doubt that there are biological and psychological differences between males and females. However, the Creator, according to Scripture, in His utmost wisdom, created the sexes with the clear purpose of having a holistic companionship and partnership and governing the earth.

It was never God's intention for the man to usurp his authority, be disrespectful, or be emotionally and physically abusive to the beautiful woman given to him.

(3) The creation narrative supports the belief that the set of physical differences between individuals who are male and female occurs as a binary. According to the Creator's intent and purpose recounted in Genesis 1:26–27, God fashioned an image converter according to the male type of humankind and an image converter according to the female type of humankind. God brought them together in the garden, where they engaged in the social decree, including reproduction and procreation, and aptitude for the agriculture of humans' successful thriving (Genesis 1:28 NRSV).

Elohim the Creator's formation of humanity as a binary being was not unique but followed the pattern of binary creation narrated in Genesis 1–2. According to Gregg R. Allison and Andreas J. Köstenberger in the book *The Holy Spirit*, the authors observe the following binaries found in the creation narrative: nothing and something, creator and creature, heaven and earth, light and darkness, dry land and water, sun and moon, good and evil, etc.

Furthermore, Genesis 2:7, in its explanation of the creation story of humankind, articulates, "Then the Lord God formed the man out of the dust from the ground and breathed the breath of life into his nostrils, and the man became a living being." Correspondingly,

Genesis 2 illuminates the creation of woman: "So the Lord God caused a deep sleep to come over the man, and he slept. God took one of his ribs and closed the flesh at that place. Then the Lord God made the rib he had taken from the man into a woman and brought her to the man" (Genesis 2:21–22 NRSV). Similarly, in connection to the creation of humankind as male and female, Genesis 6:19 enunciates, "And of every living thing, of all flesh, you shall bring two of every kind into the ark, to keep them alive with you; they shall be male and female" (Genesis 6:19 NRSV).

The Old Testament asserts that God created man and woman in the image of God, equal in worth, value, civil liberties, and individuality. However, sin has distorted God's design order (Genesis 1:26–27; Galatians 3:28).

Chartier, Jan, and Myron Raymond Chartier, in the article "Humanity Created in God's Image as Male and Female," articulate, "Male and female are made for love… One key to understanding the special place of being created as male and female is that humanity is made for loving relationship." This is a profound truth because, in reality, intimate partner violence is contradictory to the Creator's intention for the unification of male and female, who were both made to engage in a loving, affectionate, and harmonious relationship.

Nathan Jastram, in the article entitled "Man as Male and Female: Created in the Image of God," explains, "The simplest and most comprehensive definition of the image of God is that it means 'to be like God.'" Nathan is correct! Constructed upon Scripture, all human beings are created with the DNA of the Creator and, as such, have the inherent potential to be like God: to be creative, produce, and be productive. Male and female are created equally with the same right to live in freedom and to achieve self-determination. Every human being was formed to be like God with intellect and creativity. All people are made in the image of God, and every human being is endowed with dignity by God and should be treated with respect and honor.

According to the New Testament account, Jesus affirms Old Testament teachings and traditions, which express the same binary in the creation of the human race as "male and female" (Matthew

19:4). The apostle Paul argues, "There is no longer Jew or Greek, there is no longer slave or free, there is no longer male and female; for all of you are one in Christ Jesus" (Galatians 3:28). This is why all spirit-formed believers should stand against racism, sexism, and all other forms of oppression.

Michelle A. Gonzales, in her book *Created in God's Image: An Introduction to Feminist Theological Anthropology*, suggests that the patriarchal interpretation of the Genesis accounts of male and female has legitimized women's secondary status within the Christian tradition. However, biblical teachings oppose gendercide, and this is the fundamental reason the Word of God opposes gender inequality and violence against women. Furthermore, the terms *male* and *female* are used as a pair of distinctions; both male and female were created in the image of God the Creator. Different but complementary, distinct but partners, united together to reflect the glory of God on the earth.

Chartier, Jan, and Myron Raymond Chartier explain, "Another key to understanding humanity's image of God identity is that persons are made to exercise responsible dominion over the rest of God's creation." The woman was given as a gift to the man, and she is essential for the purpose of being coruler of earth. Gender is a social construction. *Gender* is defined by *Webster's Dictionary* as "the behavioral, cultural, or psychological traits typically associated with one sex" or "the characteristics of women, men, girls, and boys that are socially constructed." God created male and female, both crowned with authority, equal in essence, equal in dignity, equal in value, and equal in worth.

(4) Scripture indicates that the physical body is integral to humanity's image. In the context of Genesis 1, male and female are classifications of biological or assigned sex. These terms refer to anatomy, compared to gender, which includes societal sets of expectations defining gender identity and role. Genesis 1:27 refers to biological sex, not to the cultural, social, and psychological aspects of being male or female. Furthermore, the instruction given by the Creator was to be "fruitful and multiply," or, in other words, to reproduce,

which requires the ovum from the female and the sperm from the male (Genesis 1:28 NRSV).

Verse 27 refers to sex, not gender identity, using the Hebrew words in Genesis 1:27 for *male* (zakar) and *female* (neqebah) (Genesis 1:27 NRSV). According to the teaching of Scripture, it is clear that human beings are identified as male or female. The Hebrew word for *image* used in Genesis 1:27 is *tselem*, which means "shape, figure, or resemblance" and exclusively refers to likeness throughout the Old Testament. Similarly, in Genesis 5, "When Adam had lived one hundred thirty years, he became the father of a son in his likeness, according to his image, and named him Seth" (Genesis 5:3 NRSV). This association defines the term as a perfect physical statue or copy of a nonphysical being.

(5) Scripture affirms in the creation story that humanity was created in the image of God. According to Marc Cortez in his book, *ReSourcing Theological Anthropology: A Constructive Account of Humanity in the Light of Christ*, the creation story in Genesis 1 implies that the Creator God's molding of humankind in the image of God is "a declaration that God intended to create human persons to be physical means through which he would manifest his own divine presence in the world." Furthermore, Dr. J. Richard Middleton, in his book *The Liberating Image: The Imago Dei in Genesis 1*, concludes that the divine declaration that humanity was created in "God's image" ought to reveal "visibility and bodiliness" as central insights about what it means for humanity to be made in the image of God.

To be human is much more than having a physical body; Scripture teaches that humanity is composed of both a physical and a spiritual constituent. Therefore, the term *image* emphasizes human anatomy. In Psalm 139, the psalmist David, the King of Israel, articulates, "I praise you, for I am fearfully and wonderfully made. Wonderful are your works; that I know very well. My frame was not hidden from you, when I was being made in secret, intricately woven in the depths of the earth" (Psalm 139:14–15). Male and female were exceptionally made with different sex organs, hormones, and personalities, yet equal in the Creator's sight.

Misconceptions by many in society, some educational establishments, and other religious communities about male dominance have influenced the behaviors of males and contributed to intimate partner violence relationships. This conflicts with God's purpose for human beings to live in peace and harmony, for male and female to achieve love, respect, gender equality, partnership, and cooperation in caring for each other and the planet earth.

Created Equal in the Image of God

Both male and female display the glory of
God's image with equal brilliance.
—Dane Ortlund, senior pastor,
Naperville Presbyterian Church, Naperville, Illinois

Within the context of perceived male dominance, we would, at the very least, be in perfect order to ask one question: *does the Bible require men and women to be viewed with different levels of importance in the church?* The Old Testament does not provide us with the final and indisputable answer to this question. Yet both proponents and opponents of females as elders in the church often look to the Old Testament for whatever evidence they proffer to buttress their argument.

Let us briefly refer to how Jesus subjected the question of divorce to analysis for His first-century Jewish audience. What Jesus did was cite the account of creation in Genesis to show how it was "in the beginning."

"And He answered and said to them, 'Have you not read that He who made them at the beginning "made them male and female," and said, "For this reason a man shall leave his father and mother and be joined to his wife, and the two shall become one flesh"?'"

(Matthew 19:4–5). Certain facts are indisputable. Genesis gives the most authentic account of the creation of male and female, because of which that account should tell us something useful about God's original concept for males and females. Also, we are given an accurate glimpse of what the ideal was before sin arrived to distort the relationship between the sexes.

In the beginning, God made them *male* and *female*, as Jesus clearly stated. Since it was this concept of creation that set a pattern for marriage, we can reasonably assume that it also sets a pattern for other forms of relationships between male and female. The initial pattern is explained in Genesis 1:26–27: "Then God said, 'Let Us make man in Our image, according to Our likeness; let them have dominion over the fish of the sea, over the birds of the air, and over the cattle, over all the earth and over every creeping thing that creeps on the earth.' So God created man in His own image; in the image of God He created him; male and female He created them." Let us note that there is a plural connotation to the usage of the word *man*, suggesting that "man" means both male and female.

Genesis 5:2 says, "He created them male and female, and blessed them and called them Mankind in the day they were created." The word *mankind* clearly includes male and female. Some scholars think it is significant that God names the human race by one sex, *man*. In other parts of Genesis where God refers to Adam, the name does not appear to mean only male, but also refers to females. We can immediately infer that male authority is *not* really God's design. Equality is His design and intent.

Both male and female are made in God's image. Genesis 9:6 says, "Whoever sheds man's blood, by man his blood shall be shed; for in the image of God He made man." Clearly, *man* in this verse does not refer exclusively to man as male, but *man* as male and female. In fact, the New Revised Standard Version of the Bible renders the verse as follows: "Whoever sheds the blood of a human, by a human shall that person's blood be shed; for in his own image God made humankind." Although some people might argue about what "the image of God" means, it is generally agreed among both conservative and liberal scholars that men and women are both made in the image of God. Most conservatives even agree with the famous theological scholar Dane Ortland when he says, "Both male and female display the glory of God's image with equal brilliance."

I refer to Genesis 1:26 again: "Then God said, 'Let Us make man in Our image, according to Our likeness; let them have dominion over the fish of the sea, over the birds of the air, and over the cattle, over all the earth and over every creeping thing that creeps on the earth.'" Let us note that both male and female were assigned to rule over the earth and its animals. Therefore, although God made male and female distinct and different from one another, this passage says nothing about male and female having different roles. Genesis 1:28–29 says, "Then God blessed them, and God said to them, 'Be fruitful and multiply; fill the earth and subdue it; have dominion over the fish of the sea, over the birds of the air, and over every living thing that moves on the earth.' And God said, 'See, I have given you every herb that yields seed which is on the face of all the earth, and every tree whose fruit yields seed; to you it shall be for food.'" That was, and has been, how matters were arranged for mankind. The instructions were given equally to male and female. Both male and female were given the command to reproduce and to rule. Both male and female were given limitless latitude to eat from every fruit-bearing tree.

The second chapter of Genesis focuses on the creation of human beings. It begins with a land that is totally barren. There was no rain, and neither were there plants nor human beings. "Before any plant of the field was in the earth and before any herb of the field had grown. For the Lord God had not caused it to rain on the earth, and there was no man to till the ground" (Genesis 2:5). The next verse says that God "formed the man from the dust of the ground." Then God planted a garden, caused trees to grow in that garden, and then He installed the man there, to take care of the garden, warning him not to eat from one particular tree. "And the Lord God commanded the man, saying, 'Of every tree of the garden you may freely eat; but of the tree of the knowledge of good and evil you shall not eat, for in the day that you eat of it you shall surely die.'" (Genesis 2:16–17). Subsequently, God declared, "It is not good for the man to be alone. I will make a helper suitable for him" (Genesis 2:18).

At this point, I invite you to note that, in contrast to the rest of creation being called "good," scripture appears to highlight that it was "not good" for the man to be all alone, by himself. Clearly, therefore, God intended that man would be a social being. The question now is, does "suitable helper" even remotely imply that the woman was created to be a *servant* to the man? Does "suitable helper" even remotely imply that the man should *trample upon* the woman? Does "suitable helper" even remotely imply that the man should so lord it over the woman that he ends up disrespecting her? The answers to those questions are a definite and resounding "No!" Even the Hebrew word for *helper* is more commonly applied to *God* as a helper of man, as we can read in Exodus 18:4, "And the name of the other was Eliezer; for he said, 'The God of my father was my help, and delivered me from the sword of Pharaoh.'" Therefore, the word *helper* cannot, and does not, presume or connote lesser authority, as God is not subordinate to anyone. The woman could "help" the man by working as his equal. The point being made in Genesis is simply that the woman is "suitable" for the man, being the same kind of being.

A further point that is obviously being made is that the man was incomplete without the woman. The verse says nothing about authority. Although Apostle Paul writes that the woman was made for the man, "Nor was man created for the woman, but woman for the man" (1 Corinthians 11:9), he still goes on to conclude that men and women are mutually dependent. "Nevertheless, neither is man independent of woman, nor woman independent of man, in the Lord" (1 Corinthians 11:11). There is no reference to inferiority or hierarchy whatsoever. Genesis tells us that after God created the animals, He brought them to the man so that the man would give them names. So the man named the animals. Yet no "suitable helper" was found for the solitary man among those animals. None of the animals was an appropriate partner. Obviously, God had known this ahead of time. We can, therefore, conclude that the exercise of naming the animals helped the man to arrive at the awareness that he was not like the animals and that he, unlike the animals already created, did not have a partner.

Once He had made man aware of his need for a partner, God put him to sleep, took one of his ribs, and fashioned a woman out of it. This tells us that although the man was made from the ground, the woman had a human origin. Definitely, this emphasizes her organic unity with the man. God brought the woman to the man, and the man declared, "This is now bone of my bones and flesh of my flesh; she shall be called woman, for she was taken out of man." These poetic expressions were the first recorded words of the man, and they expressed his joy at discovering the suitable partner that he needed. The two people, although different, were the same flesh. These words are an expression of similarity, not of hierarchy. Although it is often noted that because the man named the woman, just as he had earlier named the animals, this is supposedly an indicator of authority, this is not necessarily so. Naming does not always indicate authority. When Adam named the woman, the point being emphasized in the text is how much like Adam she was.

Genesis 2:24 says, "For this reason a man will leave his father and mother and be united to his wife, and they will become one flesh." Curiously, the injunction to leave one's parents is addressed to the man, not the woman. The couple becomes a new family, totally free of the authority of the man's father and mother. This indicates that the man's primary responsibility is to his wife, not his parents, and similarly, the woman's primary responsibility is to her husband, not her parents. Strikingly, the verse presumes nothing about the authority of one person over another. The second chapter of Genesis gives clear distinctions between the man and the woman. The man was made first, given a job in the garden, warned about the forbidden fruit, given the assignment of naming the animals, and he responded with joy to his God-given companion. The woman, on the other hand, is given no role in this chapter. The movement in this chapter of Genesis is not from *superior to inferior* but from *incompleteness to completeness*. The man was created first, and it is often concluded that God gave him authority over the woman. Yet we cannot safely make this assumption. Throughout Genesis, we see that the firstborn does not always lord it over younger siblings.

In his First Letter to the Corinthians, Apostle Paul says that a woman should cover her head when prophesying, but a man should not, for "woman is the glory of man. For man did not come from woman, but woman from man; neither was man created for woman, but woman for man." This statement by Paul, not surprisingly, has generated a lot of controversy in Christendom. Yet it is clear that Paul is saying that although men and women in the Corinthian society of his day may prophesy, they must do it in slightly different ways. *He is by no means addressing the relative authority of men and women, nor the authority of what they say, but only the appearance of the person saying it.* Furthermore, Paul weakens any argument of the superiority of the man because he was created first by observing that male-female relationships are transformed in the Lord: "Nevertheless, neither is man independent of woman, nor woman independent of man, in the Lord. For as woman came from man, even so man also comes through woman; but all things are from God" (1 Corinthians 11:11–12). These verses resonate with equality in the Lord, and they remind us that although the first woman came from the first man, all subsequent men have come from women. We can ultimately surmise that Paul, in his pronouncement on the covering of one's head, does not imply that men are given authority over women. Rather, he allows women to do the same as men, advising appropriate conformity with cultural norms.

Now let us look at Genesis 2:21–23: "And the LORD God caused a deep sleep to fall on Adam, and he slept; and He took one of his ribs, and closed up the flesh in its place. Then the rib which the LORD God had taken from man He made into a woman, and He brought her to the man." Interestingly, a lot of interpreters have offered suggestions about the symbolism implied in the story of the rib. For example, Matthew Henry, best known for his six-volume biblical commentary *Exposition of the Old and New Testaments*, otherwise known as the Matthew Henry Bible Commentary, wrote, "Woman is not made of a man's head to climb over him, she is not made of his feet to be trampled on, but from his rib to be by his side as an equal, under his arm to be protected and close to his heart to be loved."

All of Christendom is in perfect agreement that, despite the male-dominated culture of His day, Jesus treated women very well. He treated them with respect. He was both sensitive and deferential to their needs. He employed the feminine gender as good examples of faith and included them in His ministry in several significant ways. Women are prominent in the story of Jesus. In any case, He was born of a woman. He also had numerous interactions with women and was seen first by women after His resurrection. As far as the Gospel goes, Jesus imparted little or no specific teaching on male and female *roles*. He never explicitly taught women to submit to men, nor did He explicitly declare that they were equal in every way. However, He did espouse on marriage. The Pharisees had asked Him, "Is it lawful for a man to divorce his wife for just any reason?" (Matthew 19:3). Obviously, their question referred to the interpretation of Deuteronomy 24:1, which says, "When a man takes a wife and marries her, and it happens that she finds no favor in his eyes because he has found some uncleanness in her, and he writes her a certificate of divorce, puts it in her hand, and sends her out of his house."

In those days, some teachers of the law argued that a man could divorce his wife if she displeased him in any way, while others taught that a man could divorce only if the wife did something indecent. Jesus responded by quoting Genesis, basically teaching that God intended marriage to last for life and that people should not break their vows. Moses allowed divorce, even for "indecency," because the people had hard hearts. "He said to them, 'Moses, because of the hardness of your hearts, permitted you to divorce your wives, but from the beginning it was not so'" (Matthew 19:8). For His usual demeanor, Jesus was surprisingly strict. "So He said to them, 'Whoever divorces his wife and marries another commits adultery against her. And if a woman divorces her husband and marries another, she commits adultery'" (Mark 10:11–12). In the Jewish world, only men could initiate divorce, putting women at a disadvantage. Jesus obviously sought to remove this male advantage. Further, He said that men could be guilty of adultery if they married another woman, which was something that the laws of Moses did not explicitly declare. Jesus makes clear that the prohibition on divorce applies equally to women. In fact, Roman law allowed women to initiate divorce. In his book *Women in Ministry*, Thomas R. Schreiner writes, "Jesus upheld the dignity of women by speaking out against divorce, which particularly injured women in the ancient world."

In another book, *Women in the Life and Teachings of Jesus*, James A. Borland writes, "In his treatment of divorce…Jesus clearly regards women not as property but as persons. They have legitimate rights and should be respected."

In the Sermon on the Mount, Jesus said, "Whoever looks at a woman to lust for her has already committed adultery with her in his heart" (Matthew 5:28). Jesus said it was adultery to even desire another woman, whether she was married or not. Jewish rabbis were well aware of the existence of lust, but they usually accused women of being seductive. Jesus, on the other hand, blamed the men. As far as He was concerned, the solution to lust is not to restrict women, but for men to restrict their own thoughts. Although this teaching refers to a male, as rules usually were, I believe that it also applies to females, meaning that a woman who looks lustfully at a man has also committed adultery in her heart. Therefore, the panacea is not to segregate the sexes, but to control their thoughts.

Jesus freely employed women as illustrations in His teachings. In many of His illustrations, Jesus presents women as positive role models of faith, which men should follow. The following are examples:

1. The woman mixing yeast into dough is presented as an illustration of the way the kingdom of God works. "The kingdom of heaven is like leaven, which a woman took and hid in three measures of meal till it was all leavened" (Matthew 13:33).
2. The widow of Zarephath. Jesus used her as an example of a Gentile whom God favored. "…but to none of them was Elijah sent except to Zarephath, in the region of Sidon, to a woman who was a widow" (Luke 4:26).
3. The woman who found the coin she had lost. "Or what woman, having ten silver coins, if she loses one coin, does not light a lamp, sweep the house, and search carefully

until she finds it? And when she has found it, she calls her friends and neighbors together, saying, 'Rejoice with me, for I have found the piece which I lost!' Likewise, I say to you, there is joy in the presence of the angels of God over one sinner who repents" (Luke 15:8–10). In this parable, the woman plays the role of God, just as the shepherd did in the preceding parable and the father does in the following parable.

4. A widow who gave everything she had. "And He looked up and saw the rich putting their gifts into the treasury, and He saw also a certain poor widow putting in two mites. So He said, 'Truly I say to you that this poor widow has put in more than all; for all these out of their abundance have put in offerings for God, but she out of her poverty put in all the livelihood that she had'" (Luke 21:1–4). On that day, while the golden coins of the wealthy merchants were making a lot of noise as they jingled their way into the offering boxes, the poor widow's mites could be heard as they made music of a celestial nature in heaven.

Jesus never denied that His own mother was blessed. But He made it clear that the real blessing is given to those who hear the word of God and obey it. A woman's spiritual worth is based on her response to God, not on performing biological functions. Women are saved by faith, not by bearing children. Christ never belittled the role of a mother, but He definitely refused to limit a woman's horizon to nurturing family and cooking. He made a similar point when people told Him that His mother and brothers wanted to speak to Him. He replied that the disciples were His real family. He said, "Whoever does the will of my Father in heaven is my brother and sister and mother." Clearly, Jesus implies that spiritual response is more important than biological origin. He expanded His response to include "sister," even though the original comment did not mention sisters, implying that women were spiritually on an equal footing with men.

CHAPTER 7

Perceptions on the Role of Women

The woman was made of a rib out of the side of
Adam; not made out of his head to rule over him,
nor out of his feet to be trampled upon by him, but
out of his side to be equal with him, under his arm to
be protected, and near to his heart to be beloved.
—Matthew Henry, author,
Matthew Henry's Commentary on the Bible

From the beginning of Christianity, women have often found greater affirmation and liberation in the Church than within the prevailing culture in which they find themselves. Yet in many cases, the same Church has totally failed them by departing from the Bible, which sees males and females as of equal worth. During its early years, Christianity propagated a unique brand of spiritual unity that, at the very least, potentially mitigated the draconian nature of Roman law, which regarded women as non-citizens with little or no legal rights. The entire socio-legal system was replete with gross inequality and feminine exclusion. For instance, while adultery by men was assumed to be the acceptable norm, adultery by women was punishable by death.

This continued into the Middle Ages, an era in which society at large assumed women would only marry and bear many children. Indeed, among the elite, parents often arranged or even forced marriages on their daughters. Monastic life offered many women an attractive alternative. This was a life of devotion, scholarship, travel, spiritual fellowship, and equal dialogue with church leaders. Yet that culture was by no means validated by the ideals of the early Church, a fact eloquently captured in the words of Apostle Paul, *"Be subject to one another in the fear of Christ" (Ephesians 5:21).* Indeed, women did gain some status "in Christ" and filled many key roles within the Church.

I will make a credible attempt to examine biblical evidence on the role of women in the apostolic Church. Various women played key roles within the work of the Church, but few were given titles, just as few men had titles. It is important to note that, although women were important in the leadership of the early Church, the Bible does not provide sufficient specifics. In many cases, one must read between the lines to see the roles they played.

The first mention of women is in Acts 1:14, which states that the original nucleus of the Church included the apostles, who all continued with one accord in prayer and supplication, *"with the women and Mary the mother of Jesus, and with His brothers." The women* might have been the apostles' wives or the women who followed Jesus. Later, Peter spoke on the fulfillment of Joel's prophecy, *"And it shall come to pass in the last days, says God, That I will pour out of My Spirit on all flesh; Your sons and your daughters shall prophesy, Your young men shall see visions, Your old men shall dream dreams. And on My menservants and on My maidservants I will pour out My Spirit in those days; And they shall prophesy" (Acts 2:17–18).* In this early Church meeting, God caused *women* to speak in tongues and prophesy in a place where *men and women* had gathered to pray and worship. In other words, women were not sidelined in the grand scheme of things.

The woman named Lydia starts to receive prominent mention in Acts 16. In *Philippi,* women came to the *"place of prayer"* outside the city. Lydia, a wealthy woman, was a believer who invited the apostles to her home, where Paul and his companions were treated to her gracious hospitality. After Paul cast a demon out of a slave girl, he was beaten, thrown into jail, rescued by an earthquake, and befriended by the jailer. Shortly before Paul and Silas left the city, they repaired to Lydia's house, where they met with the brothers and encouraged them. Since Lydia was a successful businesswoman and hosted the meeting, we can safely conclude that she was influential in the Church, although she was not given a formal title.

In *Thessalonica,* Paul preached at the synagogue, persuading some of the Jews and a sizable number of God-fearing Greeks and prominent women. In *Athens,* a woman named Damaris became a believer. Acts 18 tells us that in *Corinth,* Paul met Aquila and Priscilla, Jews who had been forced to leave Rome. They were tentmakers, and Paul worked with them for a while. They traveled to Ephesus with Paul. After Apollos came to Ephesus, Priscilla and Aquila invited him to their home and exhaustively preached about God to him. When both husband and wife are mentioned in Greek writings, the man is usually named first. Luke, on the other hand, in his narrative in Acts, named Priscilla first. This might indicate that she was the more prominent of the couple. This might also suggest that Priscilla had an astute grasp of Christian doctrine. Finally, Luke mentions that four daughters of Philip prophesied in Acts 21:9, presumably on a regular basis: *"Now this man had four virgin daughters who prophesied."*

Apostle Paul mentions Phoebe in Romans 16. Phoebe was a notable woman in the Church of Cenchrea who was trusted by Paul to deliver his letter to the Romans. In introducing and commending her for faithfully discharging this assignment, Paul calls her "a *diakonos* of the church in Cenchrea." Paul refers to her both as a "servant" or *diakonos,* which is Greek for *deacon,* and as a *prostatis,* Greek for helper or patron of many. Notably, this is the only place in the New Testament where a woman is specifically referred to with these two distinctions. Paul introduces Phoebe as his emissary to the Church in Rome, and because they are not acquainted with her, Paul provides them with her credentials: *"I commend to you Phoebe our sister, who is a servant of the church in Cenchrea, that you may receive her in the Lord in a manner worthy of the saints, and assist her in whatever business she has need of you; for indeed she has been a helper of many and of myself also" (Romans 16:1–2).* Phoebe was apparently a woman of solid means who helped take care of some of the poorer believers in Cenchrea. She had some business in Rome, and Paul asked her to carry his letter to the believers there. In turn, he asks the believers to help her accomplish whatever she came to do. She was a trusted person who was obviously well respected in the Church at Cenchrea.

Clearly, women had various important functions in the early Church. These roles included *teaching, prophecy, the provision of financial support, and gospel work.* Various people in the early Church are called apostles, but rarely is anyone, male or female, given any other title. We know the names of only two men who are called elder; Peter and John call themselves elders in *1 Peter 5:1* and *2 John 1*, and one woman who was called a deacon; Phoebe was probably called a *deacon* in *Romans 16:1.* Since titles are rarely given, it is more important to look at what people did and not what titles they held. It is also significant to see that in several cases, women worked alongside men in spreading the gospel, and the same Greek words are used to describe their work as are used for male leaders.

Now let us take the narrative to the present-day Church. Linda Hartz Rump, a highly respected divinity scholar, in a closer study of church history, concluded that for many church women, *"the Church has fallen far from the standards of the scriptures, which teaches that both genders are equally valuable."* She explains that, although in the early years of Christianity, the Church taught a doctrine of spiritual unity between male and female, there was yet a great deal of inequality in the culture recorded in the scriptures. For example, for men, adultery was assumed to be the acceptable norm while for women, adultery was punishable by death (John 8:1–11). It was in the context of this culture that Paul wrote, *"There is neither Jew nor Greek, there is neither slave nor free man, there is neither male nor female; for you are all one in Christ Jesus" (Galatians 3:28).* Apart from salvation for mankind, the death of Jesus opened the door of liberation for both males and females, which is the spiritual unity of the Body of Christ, and women gained some status "in Christ," filling key roles within the Church.

However, many church fathers of the *Patristic Period* did not view women favorably. The word "*Patristic*" derives from the Latin word *patres* (Fathers), and is a term used historically to describe the time and writings of the Church Fathers. These were the early Christians who defended the Gospel against misunderstandings and rival doctrines, wrote sermons and extensive commentaries on the Bible, recorded relevant events into Church history, and brought together the best thought of their age with their own Christian faith. That era began sometime around the end of the 1st century, when the New Testament was almost completed, and ended toward the close of the 8th century.

The reason why the fathers of the *Patristic Period* had such a jaundiced view of women was probably due to the views held by the very early church fathers. It was because of Eve, Tertullian, the influential teacher argued, and therefore because of all womankind, that *"God's image, man"* was condemned to death. He added, "How dare any woman think about adorning yourself over and above your tunics of skins?" The early church fathers' interpretation of The Fall, and specifically Eve's role within that narrative, mirrored Tertullian's comparison of all women to Eve, calling them *"the devil's gateway."* Tertullian was merely a product of the culture and the era in which he lived.

Similarly, in his *Literal Commentary on Genesis*, Augustine rendered a speech that promoted his belief that Adam was spiritually minded and could have been led astray by Eve. Augustine concluded, *"The woman was of small intelligence and the inferior flesh, which is the reason that through Eve the man became guilty of transgression."* I am still willing to understand that these statements were, to some degree, based on the culture of that era. What is unfortunate is that because women continue to be oppressed and blamed in certain sectors of Christendom, they are made to feel inferior. This sort of rationalization has continued, even in the traditional Christian thinking that has its roots in the cultural belief of Judaism, in which many still believe that women were created only to be the man's helper and for the reproduction of children.

Throughout biblical history, women were cast almost exclusively in the role of *homemaker*, while men had the role of *provider* and *protector*. With Jewish culture in the first century being decidedly patriarchal, wives were restricted to the home front, a married woman's place being entirely restricted to the care of the house and the family. Psalm 45:13 appears to eulogize this reality of that era: *"All glorious is the princess within her chamber; her gown is interwoven with gold."* The home, be it a palace or a two-bed apartment, was and is supposed to represent a place of love, comfort, extravagance, and security for God's daughters. Women were responsible for bearing children, rearing them, and maintaining a hospitable environment.

Dr. Zhava Glaser, who teaches biblical Hebrew as well as advanced Hebrew exegesis in the Old Testament at the Charles L. Feinberg Center, where she also teaches Jewish history and Jewish ethics, wrote, *"While a man's primary responsibility was seen as public, a woman's life was confined almost entirely within the private family sphere."* Invariably marrying young, a woman was almost always under the protection and authority of a man, who could either be her father or her husband. Most women were conditioned and programmed to believe that they could only be caregivers of the family, because of which the average woman traversed her lifetime without any personal or professional goals.

In synagogues, women had to remain in their place, separated from the men. That invariably also meant women were excluded from religious ceremonies. This was also during the lifetime of Jesus, and the culture was both oppressive and restrictive for women. There was no doubt that women were subjugated by the power of a domineering system. They had no rights as human beings and were regarded as property of their husbands. As a woman did not work outside of the home, childless widows with no sons to provide for them would often endure situations of extreme hardship. In the face of all this, Isaiah the prophet proclaims, *"Learn to do right; seek justice. Defend the oppressed. Take up the cause of the fatherless; plead the case of the widow"* (Isaiah 1:17). The Psalmist states, *"A father to the fatherless, a defender of widows, is God in his holy dwelling"* (Psalm 68:5). James adds in his New Testament writings, *"Religion that God our Father accepts as pure and faultless is this: to look after orphans and widows in their distress and to keep oneself from being polluted by the world"* (*James 1:27*). These verses indicate that Scripture documents the sufferings of the widows. Jesus came to Earth to fulfill His assignment to demonstrate the love of His Father and to liberate mankind. As stated in Luke 4:18–19, *"The Spirit of the Lord is on me, because He has anointed me to proclaim good news to the poor. He has sent me to proclaim freedom for the prisoners and recovery of sight for the blind, to set the oppressed free, to proclaim the year of the Lord's favor."*

Jesus' mission includes the liberation of those that are physically imprisoned and psychologically in bondage, and correcting the cultural restrictions placed on women. Jesus gave physical, emotional, and spiritual freedom to the oppressed, the marginalized, the lower classes, and the underprivileged people of his time.

Jennifer A. Glancy, a professor and scholar of New Testament and Early Christianity at Le Moyne College in Syracuse, New York, is an expert in the cultural history of early Christianity and women's history in antiquity. One of her case studies focused on "the dynamics of cultural complexity" in the exchanges of Jesus of Nazareth with those whom He encountered. She discovered that in New Testament times, individuals who met Jesus were representatives of a culturally complex world. She drew from the story of the woman presented in Mark 7. This woman was a non-Jewish woman, a Greek and a Syrian, whose daughter had an unclean spirit. The woman came humbly before Jesus, fell at his feet, and begged him to drive the demon out of her daughter. She was a woman from a different country, society, and cultural background. However, the woman, with an urgent need, had heard about how Jesus demonstrated a pattern of respecting women, welcoming foreigners, and associating with the poor. Jesus told her, *"First I should feed the children—my own family, (the Jews). It isn't right to take food from the children and throw it to the dogs"* (Mark 7:25–28 NLT).

In essence, Jesus was reminding the woman that His first responsibility was to His family, the Jewish people. Despite that fundamental truth, the *Deliverer* never ignored the rejected poor or displaced women. At the end of the conversation with Jesus, the woman went home and found her daughter healed (Mark 7:30). Jesus could have turned this humble lady away. Rather, He showed her love and compassion, as evidenced by the healing of her daughter. Most people who had an encounter with Jesus were representative of culturally complex worlds. In other words, they were representations of diversity, as people from all cultural backgrounds pursued Jesus. People came with their various beliefs, attitudes, languages, and behaviors, but Jesus was able to transcend all cultural barriers and extend His compassion and liberating grace to all. The Son of God was not overly concerned about gender, culture, class, or status. He demonstrated His love, empathy, and kindness to individuals from all ethnicities and statuses.

Although culture is said to define individuals, Jesus Christ transcended all known cultural norms and barriers. For example, Jesus chose to break with Jewish social norms and religious traditions whenever He interacted with females in public. In fact, He even ministered to a woman who was menstruating: *And a woman was there who had been subject to bleeding for twelve years, but no one could heal her" (Luke 8:43–48).* Verse 44 says, *"She came up behind him and touched the edge of his cloak, and immediately her bleeding stopped."* Jesus could have rebuked the woman. However, that would have cast Him in the mold of those who supported the old order of enslavement and restriction of women. Instead, Jesus demonstrated sincere compassion, respect, and empathy for the woman.

By the time Jesus walked the Earth, the culture had become even less hospitable and accepting of the needs of women. Jesus' message of the good news was the physical, emotional, and spiritual liberation of all, not just men but women as well. Professor Amy-Jill Levine, University Professor of New Testament and Jewish Studies at Vanderbilt Divinity School and College of Arts and Science, had this to say: *"Women followed Jesus for the same reason that their fathers, their sons, their husbands, and their brothers followed him: They found his message compelling."* Jesus did not disregard or reject the menstruating woman. Rather, He called her to Himself, in full knowledge of her bleeding disorder and physical disability.

Over the centuries, society has placed women in a box, and many women continue to face discrimination and oppression, even in our modern times. However, women found hope in Jesus, the great liberator. Jesus extended His love, grace, and mercy to both men and women, regardless of gender differences, cultural inequalities, marital status, or economic class. Another encounter that boldly illustrated Jesus's defiance of the cultural norms of His day was when He publicly initiated a discussion with the Samaritan woman. This woman was an outsider with an indeterminate past. Yet Jesus approached her and asked for a drink. The woman was surprised that Jesus, a Jew, would even condescend to begin a conversation with her, an outcast. After Jesus revealed all her secrets to her, the woman had a conversion experience and began to spread the word of Jesus to her community: *"Come, see a man who told me everything I ever did. Could this be the Messiah?" (John 4:29–30).*

It is my opinion that Jesus Christ was exceedingly successful in His assignment to dismantle the oppressive and male-domineering system against women. Jesus refused to treat women as objects and as inferior beings. His treatment of the oppressed and unfortunate was unquestionably opposed to the social and cultural norms of the day. The authors of the gospels confirm that the Savior treated women with respect, compassion, and dignity. God in the flesh rejected the old cultural boundaries and limitations. The Son of Man recognized the struggle and oppressive treatment of women and saw their worth, potential, and the desires of their hearts. He came to address those critical needs. The Savior extended His heart of love by placing His healing hands on the oppressed. He offered compassion, reassurance, and the promise of hope to women. God's liberator, Jesus Christ, understood that the role of women is a significant part of God's creation because women are co-heirs in God's plan for the salvation of mankind.

CHAPTER 8

The Primordial Intention of Marriage

God did not create woman from man's head,
that he should command her, nor from his feet,
that she should be his slave, but rather from
his side, that she should be near his heart.

—Myles Munroe,
The Purpose and Power of Love and Marriage

We need to be crystal clear about the fact that domestic violence occurs within the space of marital or intimate relationships, and mostly between heterosexual couples. It is also vital to understand what Scripture advises and what knowledge and enlightenment theological scholars can glean from the first book of the Bible about the first male and female interaction. Therefore, my attempt will be to examine the narrative of creation in the Book of Genesis, to facilitate an astute grasp of the purpose of *Elohim* as it relates to the two sexes He saw fit to create, and to ultimately obtain a better understanding of God's plan when He created the first man. This includes understanding His motive for fashioning woman out of man and exploring the significance of that creation.

The story of creation in Genesis contains the description of an intentional Creator who, in His infinite wisdom, formed the original humans. Motivated by love and compassion, *the Supreme Deity* created mankind with physical, social, psychological, and sexual needs. The Creator said, *"It is not good for the man to be alone. I will make a helper suitable for him"* (*Genesis 2:18 NIV*). In that season of total desolation in *time* and *place*, Adam was alone and had no other human being with whom to emotionally bond, to love and be loved, and to experience the joy of human sexuality. Additionally, Adam had no other living individual with whom he could have a rational conversation. It was out of this compelling need for friendship, companionship, and partnership that the Creator assumed the role of the first anesthesiologist and surgeon and proceeded on the first major surgical intervention to fashion out a suitable helpmate for Adam. *"At last!"* Adam exclaimed, *"This one is bone from my bone, and flesh from my flesh! She will be called 'woman,' because she was taken from 'man'"* (*Genesis 2:23 NLT*). According to Genesis 1:26, *"Then God said, 'Let us make human beings in our image, to be like us.'"*

God immediately assigned the man and the woman to the all-important task of being caretakers of the Earth to ensure the maintenance and preservation of God's beautiful creation. Genesis 1:27 repeats, *"So God created mankind in His own image, in the image of God, He created them; male and female He created them."* The word *them* refers to the two individuals who, at that time, comprised the entirety of humanity. The Creator established His position and intention on equality by delegating to both the man and woman the responsibility to have authority over the Earth. In every essence, they were partners in rulership. Male and female were created in the image of God to live in harmony and to have dominion over the Earth. *They were not created, not by the remotest stretch of the imagination, to have dominion over one another.* This emphasis is decidedly mine.

The first woman possessed the values of *self-worth* and *dignity*, and her companion, the first man, clearly understood this. Embedded in the Genesis narrative is unequivocal evidence to support the fact that Adam was well aware that Eve came out of him and that she was his equivalent in every respect, only equipped with differing, yet totally complementary, reproductive organs. Adam demonstrated his appreciation for the woman by naming her *"Eve."* The man said, *"This is now bone of my bones and flesh of my flesh; she shall be called 'woman,' for she was taken out of* man" (Genesis *2:23 NIV).* Adam named his wife Eve because she would become the progenitor or mother of all humans. In other words, man and woman were one because they were made from the same material. There is no evidence to suggest that Eve was made to feel inferior to Adam, and he, Adam, perfectly understood that she brought him companionship—a true partnership that was designed to aid their joint assignment as custodians of Earth—and the inestimable value that genuinely enriched his life.

One motivation and desire of the Creator, when He created the man and his woman, was that both of them would live in an environment of love, genuine partnership, and harmony. God ordained the institution of marriage so that the man would have a spouse and a supportive partner for progeny. This principle of a helpmate demonstrates that any man who abuses his wife does not understand the value of his partner, and an abusive husband lacks respect and love for his woman.

But what is marriage in its contemporary definition, and with due regard to its intention by God, and for man? Marriage is the *intimate union* and *equal partnership* of a man and a woman. Simple. Marriage comes to us as a special dispensation from God, who created male and female in His image so that they might become one body and be fertile and multiply. It goes without saying that, although man and woman are equal as God's children, they are created with significant differences that allow them to give themselves to each other and to receive from each other.

Marriage is both a *sacred union* and a *natural institution* because it is rooted in the divine plan of creation. In addition, the Catholic Church, for instance, teaches that the valid marriage between two baptized Christians is also a sacrament, which is a saving reality and a symbol of Christ's love for His Church.

> Husbands, love your wives, just as Christ
> also loved the church and gave Himself for her,
> that He might sanctify and cleanse her with the
> washing of water by the word, that He might

present her to Himself a glorious church, not
having spot or wrinkle or any such thing, but
that she should be holy and without blemish. So
husbands ought to love their own wives as their
own bodies; he who loves his wife loves himself.
For no one ever hated his own flesh, but nour-
ishes and cherishes it, just as the Lord does the
church. For we are members of His body, of His
flesh and of His bones. 'For this reason, a man
shall leave his father and mother and be joined
to his wife, and the two shall become one flesh.'
This is a great mystery, but I speak concerning
Christ and the church. Nevertheless, let each one
of you in particular so love his own wife as himself, and let the wife see that she respects her husband. (Ephesians 5:25–33)

In every marriage, spouses have entered into a contract with
each other. In a sacramental marriage, the couple also enters into a
covenant in which their love is sealed and strengthened by God's love.
The free consent of spouses makes a marriage. From this consent,
and from the sexual consummation of marriage, a special bond is created between husband and wife. This bond is lifelong and exclusive.
In the Church, the officiating minister, the witnesses, and the congregation are all witnesses to the exchange of consent, in the form of
the matrimonial vow, by the couple. Ultimately, in the Church, the
covenant is sealed by the officiating minister's blessing after receiving
the couple's consent. Exclusivity and faithfulness are essential to marriage because they foster and protect the purposes of marriage. These
broad purposes are *growth in mutual love between the spouses* and the
generation and raising of children, otherwise known as procreation.

The mutual love of a married couple should always be receptive
to the creation of new life. This openness is expressed powerfully in
the sexual union of husband and wife. The power to create a child
with God is at the heart of what spouses share with each other in
sexual intercourse. Mutual love includes the mutual gift of fertility.

Yet even couples who are not able to conceive or who are beyond their child-bearing years can still express openness to life. They can share their generative love with grandchildren, other children and families, and the wider community. As a result of baptism in Christ, all Christians are called to a life of holiness. When this divine calling is lived in marriage, it becomes a unique contribution to the life and mission of the Church. The family arises from marriage. Parents, children, and family members form what is called a *domestic church* or *church of the home.* This is the primary unit of the Church and the place where the Church lives in the daily love, care, hospitality, sacrifice, forgiveness, prayer, and faith of the ordinary family.

Having established this foundation, let us delve into God's specific purposes for marriage.

To validate His *first purpose*, God created the Earth and the animals. He said, *"Let Us make man in Our image, according to Our likeness; and let them rule over the fish of the sea and over the birds of the sky and over the cattle and over all the earth, and over every creeping thing that creeps on the earth."* The account continues, *"God created man in His own image, in the image of God He created him; male and female He created them"* (*Genesis 1:26–27*). God's first purpose for creating man and woman and joining them in marriage was to mirror His image on Earth. I invite you to center your attention on those words *"mirror His image."* The Hebrew word for "mirror" means to reflect God, to magnify, to exalt, and to glorify Him. Marriage is meant to reflect God's image to a world that is in dire need of seeing who He is. Because we are created in the image of God, people who wouldn't otherwise know what God is like should be able to look at us and get a glimpse of who He is.

In His *second purpose,* God seeks for us to complete each other and experience companionship. Scripture clearly outlines this second purpose for marriage: to mutually complete each other. That is why God said, *"It is not good for the man to be alone; I will make him a helper suitable for him"* (*Genesis 2:18)*. Adam was clearly isolated in the Garden of Eden, and so God created woman to eliminate that isolation. Writing to the first-century church in Corinth, Paul would eloquently echo the teachings in Genesis 2 when he asserted,

"However, in the Lord, neither is woman independent of man, nor is man independent of woman" (*1 Corinthians 11:11*). In a good marriage, a man and a woman are like a *computer* and *software*. Standing alone, the computer and software are impressive, but combined as a team, they accomplish so much more. That was exactly what God had in mind when He performed the first marriage with an original groom and bride named Adam and Eve. A couple needs each other. In other words, if a marriage is built according to God's blueprint, as the years go by, a couple gradually come to appreciate the genius of God in seemingly custom-making a couple for each other.

God's *third purpose* is to *multiply* a divine legacy. The children that are the offspring of a marriage are a line of godly descendants that are meant to carry a reflection of God's character to the next generation. God's original plan called for the home to be a sort of greenhouse; a nurturing place where children grow up to learn character, values, and integrity. Sadly, one of the tragedies of this generation is that most couples seem to be raising children that lack a sense of mission and direction. A fallout of the dislocations caused by domestic upheaval is that children are not being imparted with the importance of leaving a spiritual legacy of changed lives. One of our assignments is to impart a sense of destiny, a spiritual mission, to our children. The responsibility of a couple is to make their home a place where their children learn what it means to love and obey God. The home should be a training center to equip children to look at the needs of people and the world through the eyes of Jesus Christ. If children do not embrace this spiritual mission as they grow up, they may live their entire lives without experiencing the privilege of God using them in a significant way in the lives of others, especially their future partners.

In conclusion, we must acknowledge that God has authority over His creation. He also knows what is best for His creation. The institutions He establishes, especially marriage, are for the good of those whom He has lovingly created. That is why rejection of God's authority ends in disaster. All suffering, shame, pain, guilt, sickness, sorrow, and death can be traced back to this rejection. It is wise, therefore, for Christians to seek to understand God's Word with a view to obeying it. When the Lord Jesus was challenged about marriage, He referred His questioners back to *the beginning*. *"He said to them, 'Moses, because of the hardness of your hearts, permitted you to divorce your wives, but from the beginning it was not so'"* *(Matthew 19:8).* This indicates that God's original design for marriage remains relevant today, and that whatever the unique problems of a particular case may be, God's ideal for marriage has been clearly revealed at *the beginning.* That ideal is reflected in God's three primary purposes for marriage: *companionship, procreation,* and *moral preservation.* Moral preservation, as a divine purpose for marriage, is a result of the fall. Apostle Paul was asked whether it was better for a man to remain single or get married. His answer was that while there was nothing wrong with remaining single, yet because of the real danger of moral failure, each man should have his own wife, and each woman should have her own husband. *"Nevertheless, because of sexual immorality, let each man have his own wife, and let each woman have her own husband"* *(1 Corinthians 7:2).*

We must always bear in mind that marriage is not a social convenience. It is a divine institution. Because of this, to redefine marriage is not within man's reserve. If there ever was a time in history when marriage could have been redefined, it was when the Lord Jesus was asked about it. However, His response was to go back to *the beginning.* We must always do the same. God's plan was to make a helpmate for Adam. God's answer to Adam's aloneness was to provide a partner who corresponded to him. That partner could not be found among the animals, for none corresponded to him. Man's partner had to be supplied by God through an act of special creation. So God *"caused a deep sleep to fall upon Adam, and he slept. Then* He *took a rib from Adam and made a woman, and brought her to the man."* Adam was put to sleep, not necessarily to demonstrate God's skill as an anesthesiologist, but to show that God *alone* bore the responsibility of selecting a partner for him. This is not to suggest that a man should not choose his own wife, but that God has decreed that the wife for any man must be a woman. A man has freedom of choice as to whom he marries, but that freedom is within clearly defined boundaries.

Finally, God's choice was accepted. *"This is now bone of my bones, and flesh of my flesh: she shall be called Woman, because she was taken out of Man."* The removal of a rib, followed by the presentation of a wife, is a parable of the relationship between a husband and his wife. He is incomplete without her and is completed by her. *"Therefore shall a man leave his father and his mother, and shall cleave unto his wife: and they shall be one flesh."* The *one flesh* relationship is a union made by God. The physical intimacy of husband and wife within marriage expresses this oneness. God intends marriage to reflect the union between Christ and His Church. *"This is a great mystery,"* wrote Paul, *"but I speak concerning Christ and the church"* *(Ephesians 5:32).* Adam represents the Lord Jesus, and Eve represents the Church. Adam is put to sleep and, as a result, has a bride. So the Lord Jesus died at Calvary, and the fruit of His death is His bride, the Church. The oneness between Christ and His Church is also emphasized, *"For we are members of his body, of his flesh, and of his bones."* The Church is described as *"His body, the fullness of Him that filleth all in all."* Marriage, as God intended it, should be honored. It reflects, in the physical realm, the most glorious of spiritual relationships. That spiritual relationship is desecrated as soon as a man visits violence, physical or emotional, upon his wife.

CHAPTER **9**

The Legacy of Oppression

The ultimate tragedy is not the oppression
and cruelty by the bad people, but the
silence over that by the good people.
—Martin Luther King Jr.

When God decided that mankind had become too sinful and must be wiped off the Earth, He chose Noah, a pious man, for a great task. Noah would build an ark large enough to hold the members of his immediate family and breeding pairs of every animal. When the task was completed, Noah and his family would witness God's wrath in the form of a flood of apocalyptic proportions.

To express matters clearly, when God beheld the corruption of the Earth and determined to destroy it, He gave Noah a divine warning of the impending disaster and made a covenant with him, promising to save him and his family. Noah was instructed to build an ark, and in accordance with God's instructions, he took into the ark male and female specimens of all the world's species of animals, from which the stocks might be replenished. Consequently, the entire surviving human race descended from Noah's three sons.

Despite the Great Flood that saw to the destruction of Earth's population, excluding Noah and his family, the repopulation of the earth did nothing to change the violent, lustful, and sinful nature of

67

people. Even Noah himself, after obeying the dominion mandate, went out from the ark to bring in a grape harvest, but now let his guard down and was caught up in the sin of drunkenness. In fact, the first mention of wine in the Bible is associated with Noah's shame, who got drunk, naked, and was disgraced (Genesis 9:21).

We have another example of perversity in ancient Egypt. The mighty and oppressive powers of the Egyptian dynasties were a demonstration of Egypt's dominance of the ancient world. The Book of Exodus is, for all practical purposes, a description of the 450-year enslavement of the people of Israel in Egypt. The Egyptians created a system of brutal and merciless injustice and oppression that was unleashed on the Israelite slaves and the helpless women who were poor, destitute, and oppressed. The Israelites cried out to the God of their ancestors. The third chapter of Exodus relates the encounter of Moses with the God of Israel.

"The Lord said, 'I have indeed seen the misery of my people in Egypt. I have heard them crying out because of their slave drivers, and I am concerned about their suffering'" *(Exodus 3:7).* The translation of this passage is that the ears of the Creator heard the cries of the downtrodden. The first chapter of Exodus had earlier referenced the growing fear of the Egyptians. Exodus 1:8–12 describes this apprehension:

> Now there arose a new king over Egypt, who did not know Joseph. And he said to his people, "Look, the people of the children of Israel are more and mightier than we; come, let us deal shrewdly with them, lest they multiply, and it happen, in the event of war, that they also join our enemies and fight against us, and so go up out of the land." Therefore they set taskmasters over them to afflict them with their burdens. And they built for Pharaoh supply cities, Pithom and Raamses. But the more they afflicted them, the more they multiplied and grew. And they were in dread of the children of Israel.

The Pharaoh had become disturbed by the growing population of the Israelites in Egypt, and he instituted slavery as a means of curtailing their influence. The lamentations of the Israelites reached God, and His heart was moved with compassion to deliver the children of Israel. God told Moses, *"The cry of the Israelites has reached me, and I have seen the ways the Egyptians are oppressing them. So now, go. I am sending you to Pharaoh to bring my people the Israelites out of Egypt" (Exodus 3:9–10).* This verse emphasizes that the cry of the people arrested God's attention. Therefore, God instructed Moses that it was time for him to fulfill his appointed duty, which was the liberation of the people of Israel.

This story of deliverance from *slavery* and *oppression* was not the only example of God's intervention in liberating His people. Hebrews 3:3 (NIV) states, *"Jesus has been found worthy of greater honor than Moses, just as the builder of a house has greater honor than the house itself."* Although Moses was known as a great deliverer, God sent One greater than Moses in the person of Christ Jesus to liberate mankind from all forms of social injustice and oppression, including classism, sexism, racism, and, of course, sin.

Human oppression is nothing new. The cycle of bloodshed and cruelty has existed since Cain killed Abel. There are many places in the Old Testament where the issue of oppression is addressed, and God clearly states that He will not tolerate injustice and oppression. People guilty of oppression will suffer the consequences of their actions. The Bible is clear about that. *"O house of David, this is what the LORD says: 'Administer justice every morning; rescue from the hand of his oppressor the one who has been robbed, or my wrath will break out and burn like fire because of the evil you have done, burn with no one to quench it'" (Jeremiah 21:12).* There are entire passages in the Bible where the Prophet Habakkuk cries out to God about injustices committed, and God responded by cursing these oppressors:

> Woe to him who builds his realm by unjust
> gain to set his nest on high, to escape the clutches
> of ruin! You have plotted the ruin of many peo-
> ples, shaming your own house and forfeiting your

life. The stones of the wall will cry out, and the beams of the woodwork will echo it. Woe to him who builds a city with bloodshed and establishes a town by crime! Has not the Lord Almighty determined that the people's labor is only fuel for the fire, that the nations exhaust themselves for nothing? (Habakkuk 2:9–13)

But what, exactly, is oppression? Oppression is what happens when people grow their own sense of power, comfort, and security at the expense of others. It is the use of violence, coercion, and corruption in an attempt to make life easier for the *oppressor* and harder for the *oppressed*. The Bible, however, unequivocally condemns oppression. *"Give justice to the weak and the fatherless; maintain the right of the afflicted and the destitute"* (Psalm 82:3). *"Learn to do good; seek justice, correct oppression; bring justice to the fatherless, and plead the widow's cause"* (Isaiah 1:17).

Oppression is the unjust use of power at other people's expense. It involves protecting one's power, comfort, security, and privilege at the expense of those with less of these than you. It is relatively easy to recognize oppression at the individual level. Often, it is the evil stepmother forcing a little girl to do all the housework. It might be the office manager harassing his female assistant for sexual favors. It could be the schoolyard bully taking the lunch money of a smaller boy. Very often, it is the husband subjecting the wife he vowed to love and protect to unspeakable emotional, physical, and sexual abuse. We observe oppression all around us, and we all know that oppression is wrong. At least, we know it is horribly wrong when we are the ones being oppressed. Yet undoing it is easier said than done.

How did oppression start? It started with a murder. Cain was jealous of his brother Abel and killed him. While Cain was tasked with ruling over creation, he didn't believe it was his responsibility to look out for his brother. *"Then the LORD said to Cain, 'Where is your brother Abel?' 'I don't know,' he replied. 'Am I my brother's keeper?'"* (*Genesis 4:9*). That was how it all started. People began to use violence and coercion to get their own way, pitting people at odds with the good order of the world. The cycle of oppression and violence quickly started to escalate.

A few generations later, one of Cain's descendants, Lamech, bragged to his wives about how he had become strong enough to murder anyone who so much as hurt him. *"Lamech said to his wives, 'Adah and Zillah, listen to me; wives of Lamech, hear my words. I have killed a man for wounding me, a young man for injuring me. If Cain is avenged seven times, then Lamech seventy-seven times'"* (Genesis 4:23–24). The violence approaches a climax, until all of humanity's thoughts were thoroughly and constantly evil.

To stem the evil tide, God designed the Great Flood to wash away the violent civilization, but He gave Noah, his family, and a few animals a second chance. Once again, God decided to bless humanity with power and authority over the world. But this time, God added the caveat, *"don't kill each other."* God warned that if you shed someone's blood, then someone else is going to come for you. Within a few generations, a violent warrior-king named Nimrod began to build an empire, which included the Tower of Babel. Later in the Bible, Babylon would become the icon of oppression in the world, with violence and coercion becoming part of the human condition, and with humanity now on track to build cruel, oppressive empires.

How does oppression work? Oppression works in today's world in much the same way it worked in biblical days. The powerful take more for themselves at the expense of the weak. This is done in several ways.

The first is *violence*. Being physically strong on an individual level, or militarily strong on a larger scale, allows some people to simply take what they want. It is the crudest form of oppression, and the earliest that we see in Scripture, with examples including the stories of Cain, Joseph's brothers, and Pharaoh.

The second is *coercion*. Sometimes violence isn't necessary. The threat of violence or the threat of negative consequences for not appeasing the powerful is enough to keep the weak in line. Pharaoh did this when keeping the children of Israel enslaved by constantly increasing their work quotas.

The third is *corruption*. If you're powerful enough, you can influence or create systems to keep you automatically in power. A common way this was expressed in ancient times was through bribes. Judges had the power to pronounce rulings in courts, but rich and powerful families could bribe judges to rule in their favor.

The fourth is *veneration*. If you're really powerful, you can get people to treat you like a god. By positioning yourself as the source of everyone else's power, security, and status, you get to define what is right and what is wrong. This means your followers will do the work of oppressing those who oppose you, and the people you're oppressing might even eventually love you.

All these affect the weak in obvious ways. They are subject to fraud, abuse, slavery, rape, homelessness, and even death. Sadly, oppressive systems create a double standard, allowing the powerful to get away with things the weak would never be able to do. This wasn't just an issue with primitive civilizations. Systemic injustice is prevalent to this day. That is why, for instance, a Black wife would run to her church pastor to bemoan gross mistreatment at the hands of her husband, and the pastor would simply tell her to go back home and be submissive to her abusive husband. It is a vicious cycle. Oppressive systems self-perpetuate. The powerful grow more powerful, which makes it easier for them to take even more from the weak. Physically stronger men can oppress physically weaker women. Wealthier classes can oppress classes of lower status. Societies with more advanced technology can oppress weaker and poorer societies. There is always someone else to oppress.

Reversing oppression is difficult because, in an oppressive system, there's not much reason for the powerful people to change things. Why would someone give up their position of power? Wouldn't that just leave a power vacuum for someone else, someone less trustworthy than they? The Book of Ecclesiastes says it all. The more powerful you become in an oppressive system, the more invested you become in maintaining that system.

> If you see the oppression of the poor, and the
> violent perversion of justice and righteousness in

a province, do not marvel at the matter; for high official watches over high official, and higher officials are over them. Moreover, the profit of the land is for all; even the king is served from the field. He who loves silver will not be satisfied with silver; Nor he who loves abundance, with increase. This also is vanity. (Ecclesiastes 5:8–10)

Dismantling an oppressive system requires the ones who benefit most to sacrifice their power and comfort. That, unfortunately, is easier said than done. Incredibly, most oppressors do not even think of themselves as oppressors. In fact, oppression can often feel like doing the right thing, or at least doing the necessary thing. That is why an abusive husband might see domestic violence as instilling discipline in his wife. It is difficult for an oppressor to see any wrong in their acts of oppression, and it is almost impossible for an oppressed person to convince an oppressor that they are doing anything wrong.

God has always been, and remains, the ultimate authority who opposes prideful oppressors and helps the weak. The Old Testament rightfully anticipated a time when the Messiah, a ruler in Israel anointed by God, would put things right and claim victory over the oppressors. By the first century, the Jews lived scattered across the world, and their homeland was under the oppressive rule of the Roman Empire. During this time, Jesus arrived on the scene, and after being baptized by John the Baptist, Jesus went into the wilderness, where He was tempted by the devil. From this point onward, Jesus began to proclaim the coming of a new kingdom, the kingdom of God. This was exciting news to some of the Jews. A prophet had come from David's line, someone they assumed would violently overthrow their Roman oppressors and restore Israel to her former glory. On at least one occasion, some Jews began a movement to make Jesus king by force.

Therefore when Jesus perceived that they were about to come and take Him by force to make Him king, He departed again to the mountain by Himself alone. (John 6:15)

Jesus, however, took a different approach to establishing a kingdom. He said that His kingdom is not of this world, and so His followers don't need violence to overthrow oppressors. Jesus stopped His followers from fighting back when He was arrested. Jesus knew that He was about to die, but He reminded His followers of the cycle of violence that God had warned Noah about.

Women who experience abuse live in an environment of verbal intimidation, physical suffering, and psychological entrapment similar to the experience of slaves. Domestic violence shares many parallels with the institution of slavery, in which the abused woman is treated like an object and verbally denigrated and belittled. Women in abusive relationships, in a manner remarkably similar to enslaved people, end up struggling with feelings of powerlessness and physical anguish and remain at the mercy of their husbands.

During the time of the enslavement of the African American people, the slaves had no rights, and they were treated in a manner that totally robbed them of any innate human value and dignity. They were consistently brutalized, severely beaten, and physically whipped, while the women were savagely raped to cater to the slave master's perverse and demented pleasure. Male slaves were sold to the highest bidder, or simply hung whenever they ran afoul of their masters' instructions.

In a similar fashion, abusive relationships exist when there is an imbalance of power. Men who visit violence on women invariably possess greater physical strength and also deploy psychological fear since, more often than not, they also hold the purse strings. In abusive relationships, women are made to feel helpless, powerless, devalued, and degraded. Yet God hates oppression, and throughout Scripture, there is a plethora of evidence to support God's abhorrence of cruelty. The prophet Jeremiah proclaimed:

> This is what the Lord Almighty says: "The people of Israel are oppressed, and the people of Judah as well. All their captors hold them fast, refusing to let them go. Yet their Redeemer is strong; the Lord Almighty is His name. He will

vigorously defend their cause so that He may bring rest to their land, but unrest to those who live in Babylon." (Jeremiah 50:33–34)

God has taken an unequivocal position on oppression, injustice to the poor, and all forms of discrimination. *"'This is what the Sovereign Lord says: You have gone far enough, princes of Israel! Give up your violence and oppression and do what is just and right. Stop dispossessing my people, declares the Sovereign* Lord' " *(Ezra 45:9)*. King David wrote:

The LORD replies, "I have seen violence done to the helpless, and I have heard the groans of the poor. Now I will rise up to rescue them, as they have longed for me to do." (Psalm 12:5)

God deplores the tyranny and mistreatment of those marginalized by society. God is clear about His hatred for injustice and oppression. God is a God of love and liberation. The world's patriarchal society is built upon a system of male dominance, control, and power. It is one in which women are restricted and made to feel like second-class citizens. Worse, to add salt to their injury, they have become the victims of unceasing violence on the domestic front. It is time for it to stop.

CHAPTER 10

The Corruption of Mortal Power

Power tends to corrupt, and absolute
power corrupts absolutely.
—John Dalberg-Acton

will open this chapter by looking at the way psychologists define power. Psychologists define power in a multiplicity of ways. However, the commonly accepted definitions converge toward two aspects of power. *First,* a powerful person is one who has control over others' resources. Such resources can take many forms, including financial resources, but can also be symbolic resources, such as societal status. *Second,* someone can be said to be powerful when they have the capacity to influence someone else and stay uninfluenced by others. We often blame the behaviors of those who have power and who abuse it on the individual and their personality. This is what psychologists call a *dispositional attribution.* Yet there is more to individual and personality differences when it comes to understanding the behavior of those who hold power over others.

Acquiring power over others comes with a series of psychological consequences. The process of acquiring power can be gradual, for instance, climbing through the hierarchy of an organization, or sudden, for instance, the vice president becoming president of the United States at the sudden death of the incumbent. In either case, power seems to reduce the human capacity to appreciate the perspective of others. Even at that, the effect of power goes beyond the ability to appreciate others' perspectives. Indeed, power tends to lead people to increase their *objectification* of others. That objectification is also powerfully at the root of men wielding their power over their women to abuse them physically and emotionally.

Research conducted by Professor Tom Reader and his colleagues at the London School of Economics in the United Kingdom showed that power tends to increase one's own peculiar sense of uniqueness, such that one starts to feel different from others. Interestingly, these scholars also discovered that power seems to decrease the sense of connectedness that men have with others while it increases that same sense in women. *Is it any wonder that women tend to handle power much better, and much more humanely, in whatever capacity, than men?* Power has also been shown to affect the experience of emotions. For instance, it has been observed that people who lack power become more attuned to others' emotions, especially when living in the same physical space. Individuals who wield power, on the other hand, tend to pay less attention to the emotions of others. This is also typically seen in abusive relationships in which the men are not in the least bothered about the emotional stability of their partners.

Altogether, psychological research suggests that power creates conditions that can be favorable to behaviors such as physical and sexual abuse in a relationship. It is important to appreciate that the link between power and negative behavior is by no means an automatic one. What is possible is that power appears to trigger inappropriate behavior in those who already have a tendency to behave in that disagreeable manner.

The question is this: In the overall effort to protect Black women from domestic violence, what can be done to sensitize Black men to their abuse of power? *First*, by making them aware of the negative consequences of their perceived power. *Second*, by encouraging them to have more empathy. Since, as I already stated, power diminishes one's capacity to take the perspectives of others into consideration and to perceive others' emotions accurately, Black men need to be taught to more positively reconnect with their women.

To achieve the objective of men reconnecting more positively with women, we need to aspire to a state of affairs in which the word *power* itself will be redefined, such that *'the power of love will replace the love of power.'* That is when our world will start to know the blessings of peace. Our world seethes with hypocrisy. Though we say we prefer *love* over *power*, the way we behave in every aspect of our lives testifies totally to the contrary. Love and power are two very different things, and they are often at odds with each other. Love is about *affection* and *respect*. Power is about *control*. When real love is the motivator, people deal with each other peacefully, and force is only used in self-defense. We respect each other's rights and differences. Tolerance and cooperation govern our interactions. Suppose we wish to influence or change the behavior of an adult. This person has done us no harm and is in full command of their faculties. Love requires that we reason with them. They are free to accept or reject our overtures. If we don't seem to be succeeding in our efforts, we don't use force against them.

A mature, responsible adult neither seeks undue power over other adults nor wishes to see others subjected to anyone's controlling schemes. In a free society, the power of love ought to govern our behavior instead of the love of power. Sadly, even our politics provide us with a very bad example. Today's politics provides a sad commentary on the ascendancy of the love of power over the power of love. Society cannot sustainably continue in this self-destructive fashion. Power cannot be the answer to society's problems. Loving others can never be synonymous with diminishing their liberties. On an individual level, especially in the relationships of men with their women, there is a renewed need to take responsibility for our own actions and decisions and to impose no burdens on others that stem from our own poor judgments. We need to strengthen our character so that we can be the model of integrity that friends, family, and acquaintances will want to respect and emulate. If we believe we are *right*, we should resolve to elicit support for that *rightness* through peaceful persuasion, and not through force. We ought to sincerely commit to learning more about the principles of *love* and *liberty* so that we can convincingly defend them against the encroachments of our own abusive power. Ultimately, we should resolve to do whatever we can to replace the *love of power* with the *power of love.*

It all started with the fall of humankind in Genesis 3, an era that witnessed tremendous dysfunction, jealousy, hate, and abuse of power. Genesis 4:1–18 tells the story of the misuse of personal power by the firstborn son of Adam and Eve, Cain, who became so enraged that he descended into the impulsive outburst of anger that resulted in the first murder. The author of Genesis captures the story:

> Now Cain said to his brother Abel, "Let us
> go out to the field." While they were in the field,
> Cain attacked his brother Abel and killed him.
> (Genesis 4:8)

The murder of Abel would spell the extraordinarily dramatic emergence of violence, as never hitherto seen in the annals of creation, and what it eloquently demonstrated was just how far mankind had tragically departed from the environment of love and harmony that was the original plan and desire of God when He created Adam and Eve. It also introduced the word *violence* into the lexicon of Scripture:

> "Now the earth was corrupt in God's sight
> and was full of violence." So, God said to Noah,
> "I am going to put an end to all people, for the
> earth is filled with violence because of them. I am
> surely going to destroy both them and the earth."
> (Genesis 6:11, 13)

To put matters in accurate perspective, during the time of Noah, there was a predominant culture of hate and violence on Earth. Culture, as we now recognize it, is a way of life, and it incorporates the customs, language, religion, and traditions that are imparted to individuals through their social interactions. Children learn through their interactions with the environment, ultimately shaping their behavior. That is why the *learned behavior of violence* is passed from one generation to the next. When a young girl or boy is raised in a culture that promotes violence, one that possibly exerts no visible effort to abhor it, all that happens is that the stage is set for society to be relentlessly sucked into a vortex of violence that also inevitably enters into a vicious cycle of self-perpetuation.

By an equal token of tragedy, if a girl is unfortunate enough to witness her mother being subjected to daily verbal disparagement or physical beatings, she enters into the learning process that portrays violence as normal behavior. It is not overly surprising that many abused women tend to attract abusive partners. That is because they have been preconditioned to violence of some form or another during childhood. My own experience with domestic violence is sufficient attestation to the fact that domestic violence is incubated in the home, and then it develops the cultural tentacles that spread to invidiously cause havoc for women. In fact, the entire culture of violence develops a life of its own and creates a never-ending pattern of abuse and pain for women.

According to Elizabeth Gerhardt, professor of theology and social ethics at Northeastern Seminary, Rochester, New York, *"The underlying causes of global violence against women and girls are rooted deep in our cultures, and the scandal of this violence is symptomatic of pervasive and deep misogyny."* Culture plays a pre-eminently central role in cultivating the mindset of men and conditioning them to think that they have superiority over females. That supposed superiority is dubious power, at the very least. Additionally, the socialization of men is deeply rooted in the culture of patriarchy that is still dominant in most parts of the world, which is why award-winning author Carolyn Custis James argues, *"Male authority over women becomes a hallmark of patriarchy. Indeed, that is precisely the meaning of patriarchy."* A critical examination of the concept of male dominance reveals that men have, for millennia, wielded *power* and *control,* even in church, where women have generally also been oppressed and told that they cannot carry out the calling of God in their lives.

Patriarchal traditions are rooted in a culture in which males possess the wealth and control the land, and in which generational wealth was passed down to the firstborn son. In these circumstances, women's expectations of wealth were strictly limited to whatever they could partake in out of the largesse of their husbands' share. In the Old Testament, the land was passed onto sons, who became the husbands. For example, *"Abraham left everything he owned to Isaac" (Genesis 25:5).* Isaac, on his own part, had two sons, Esau and Jacob. Esau, as firstborn, had unquestionable entitlement to the birthright but sold his inheritance of land and cattle ownership to his younger brother Jacob (Genesis 25:29–32). Genesis 27 continues with a fascinating story. "So, he went to him and kissed him. When Isaac caught the smell of his clothes, he blessed him" (Genesis 27:27). Jacob had deceitfully received the superior blessing, one that was statutorily given to the firstborn son.

The long and short of human history is that men have always held the position of dominance, power, and authority over women. This culture of patriarchy continues to prevail in today's social systems and the structures of power. It is this patriarchal system that has resulted in many women being subjected to inequality, injustice, oppression, physical harm, and even death. By an equal extension of the truth, it is men who abuse their wives or girlfriends, in a bid to maintain dominance, power, and control over them, promoting the legacy of patriarchy. It is an open secret that many of such men actually possess the mindset that women are inferior, are mere objects for sex, and are intended to please men in any way they see fit. When all is said and done, intimate partner violence remains an abuse of power that has negatively impacted millions of women, including Black churchwomen.

CHAPTER 11

The Black Church as Arbiter

The Black Church has a tremendous responsibility
in combating domestic violence and sending
the clear message that it is not acceptable.
—Gloria White-Hammond, copastor,
Bethel American Methodist Episcopal Church, Boston

Beyond the raucous laughter and often bawdy humor, beyond the dancing, clapping, screaming, and shouting that are seemingly characteristic features of Sabbath school or Sunday service in the average Black church, is a story of kindness, fierce intelligence, struggles, successes, bitterness, and trauma that make up the entire Black experience in America. In essence, therefore, the story of the Black church is the story of the struggles that all African people experience living in America. Standing separate from the dominant white society, yet engaged in a continuing dialogue with it, the Black church evolved with numerous acts of piety and protest, faith and resistance.

The Black church has been profoundly shaped by regional differences—North and South, East and West—yet the church was, and remains, sustained and galvanized by the twin ideas of *emancipation* and *freedom*, a symbolism that depicts the African people's experience of slavery and subjugation. Today, nothing in the Black church is more reminiscent of the need for *emancipation* and *freedom* than the experience of the Black woman in the hands of the Black man in the same church.

The term *Black church* evolved from the phrase "the Negro church," the title of a pioneering sociological study of African American Protestant churches at the turn of the century by W. E. B. Du Bois, the Pan-Africanist civil rights activist. At its origin, the phrase was considered a mere academic categorization. In fact, many African Americans did not think of themselves as belonging to the Negro church, but rather described themselves according to denominational affiliations such as *Methodist*, *Baptist*, and *Presbyterian*.

Today the Black church is widely understood to include the seven major Black Protestant denominations: National Baptist Convention, National Baptist Convention of America, Progressive National Convention, African Methodist Episcopal Church, African Methodist Episcopal Zion Church, Christian Methodist Episcopal Church, and Church of God in Christ. Furthermore, the term *Black church* may also refer to individual congregations where membership is predominantly of people of African lineage or African Americans.

According to Professor Jonathan Lee Walton, president of Princeton Theological Seminary, Princeton, New Jersey, for more than three hundred years, the Black church in America has provided a safe haven for Black Christians in a nation shadowed by the legacy of slavery and a society defined by race and class. Inspired by the story of *Exodus*, African Americans *think* out, *pray* out, and *shout* out their anger and aspirations, free from the unstated and denied constraints that govern dialogue with white society. In the pulpit and in the pews, in choir lofts and Sunday schools, the Black church continues to offer affirmation and dignity to a people still searching for equality and justice and still wallowing in the hope of a more inclusive and embracing tomorrow.

Men commanded, and continue to command, the pulpits of the Black church. They also dominated, and still dominate, church power and politics. Denied the chance to preach, growing numbers of Black women found other ways to participate in religious life. They organized social services, missionary societies, early morning prayer groups, temperance associations, and reading groups. They fought for suffrage and demanded social reform. They wrote for religious periodicals that promoted traditional and old-world ideals of respectability and womanhood. Like the crusading newspaper reporter Ida B. Wells, they protested racial injustice, lynching, and violence.

Among the most influential of these Black women was a young lady named Nannie Burroughs, who served as secretary of the Women's Convention of the National Baptist Convention. In a major address to the National Baptist Convention delivered in 1920, she directly chastised Black ministers: "We might as well be frank and face the truth. While we have hundreds of superior men in the pulpits, North and South, East and West, the majority of our religious leaders have preached too much Heaven and too little practical Christian living. In many, the spirit of greed, like the horse-leech, is ever crying, 'Give me, give me, give me.' Does the absorbing task of supplying their personal needs blind leaders to the moral, social, and spiritual needs of our people?" Men, she argued, must welcome women into the affairs of government. Women must organize and educate. "There will be protest against politics in the Church," she predicted, but insisted, "It is better to have politics than ignorance." Today, the ordeal of the Black woman transcends marginalization in the church itself. It has tragically extended to the home front of the church community, in which the *spiritual leader* of the home, the husband, has transformed into the *terror master* of the same home.

From the foregoing, by the term *African American church*, or *Black church*, I clearly allude to the constellation of Protestant churches that currently, or that have historically, derived their ecclesiastical leadership from the Black clergy or principally have a larger percentage of African Americans in their membership within the United States. As I already mentioned, there is no doubt whatsoever that African American church leadership has played an exceedingly active role in issues of oppression and racial injustice. Black church leaders are renowned and held in high esteem for the prominent role they have played in the struggle for human rights, voting rights, civil rights, social equality, and the improvement of the lives of African American people.

In this regard, I can provide no finer example of Black church leadership's active involvement in the civil rights movement than Reverend Martin Luther King Jr., whose grandfather began the family's long tenure as pastors of the Ebenezer Baptist Church in Atlanta, Georgia. Martin Luther King Jr. attended segregated public schools in Georgia, graduating from high school at the age of fifteen. He received a BA degree in 1948 from Morehouse College, from which both his father and grandfather had graduated. After three years of theological study at Crozer Theological Seminary in Pennsylvania, where he was elected president of a predominantly white senior class, he was awarded the BD in 1951 and later obtained his doctorate in divinity from Boston University in 1955. It was in Boston that he met and married Coretta Scott, a young woman of uncommon intellectual and artistic attainments.

In 1954, Martin Luther King became pastor of the Dexter Avenue Baptist Church in Montgomery, Alabama. Always a strong worker for civil rights for members of his race, King was, by this time, a member of the executive committee of the National Association for the Advancement of Colored People (NAACP), the leading organization of its kind in the nation. He was ready, then, early in December 1955, to accept the leadership of the first great Negro nonviolent demonstration of contemporary times in the United States, a bus boycott that lasted 382 days. On December 21, 1956, after the Supreme Court of the United States had declared unconstitutional the laws requiring segregation on buses, Negroes and Whites rode the buses as equals. During these days of the boycott, King was arrested, his home was bombed, and he was subjected to personal abuse, but at the same time, he emerged as a Negro leader of the first rank.

In 1957, he was elected president of the Southern Christian Leadership Conference, and in the 11 -year period between 1957 and 1968, King traveled over 6 million miles and spoke over 2,500 times, appearing wherever there was injustice, protest, and action. Meanwhile, he wrote 5 books as well as numerous articles. In these years, he led a massive protest in Birmingham, Alabama, that caught the attention of the entire world, providing what he called a coalition of conscience, and inspiring his "Letter from a Birmingham Jail," a manifesto of the Negro revolution. He also planned the drives in Alabama for the registration of Negroes as voters. He directed the peaceful march on Washington, DC, of 250,000 people to whom he delivered his address "I Have a Dream." He conferred with President John F. Kennedy and campaigned for President Lyndon B. Johnson. He was arrested more than 20 times and assaulted at least 4 times. He was awarded 5 honorary degrees. He was named Man of the Year by *Time* magazine in 1963 and became not only the symbolic leader of American Blacks but also a world figure.

At the age of 35, Martin Luther King Jr. was the youngest man to have received the Nobel Peace Prize. When notified of his selection, he announced that he would turn over the prize money of $54,123 to the furtherance of the civil rights movement. On the evening of April 4, 1968, while standing on the balcony of his motel room in Memphis, Tennessee, where he was to lead a protest march in sympathy with striking garbage workers of that city, he was assassinated.

I offer this concise description of the life of Martin Luther King Jr. to highlight the significantly long journey that the African American church and its leadership have been on concerning social injustice and inequality. Furthermore, the African American church has played a prominent role in addressing issues fundamentally affecting African American families while exerting effort to preserve the traditional values of the Black community. The Black church has stood as a pillar of the local community, establishing schools, feeding the hungry, and housing the homeless. The African American church has been, and still is, the place where important issues concerning the African American community are addressed.

Despite all these, many Black couples in the church struggle in silence with intimate partner violence. It is nothing short of a sad commentary that, on Sunday mornings, many victims and perpetrators sit together in the pews of churches suffering silently.

According to Lee H. Bowker, a scholar in the field of domestic violence, "Clergy have made major mistakes in the management of domestic violence disclosures; many pastors are uninformed on issues related to handling reports made by abused women who disclosed that they had been subjected to intimate partner violence." Of pertinently shameful commentary, many church leaders hide under the cover of denial, while others use avoidance and simply look the other way instead of attending to reports of intimate partner violence. Bowker expresses the view, "In spite of church leaders' desire to help abused parishioners, some clergy often minimize the problem of family violence and regularly express optimistic views about abusers; often church leaders have given harmful advice to victims." In many cases, pastors employ scripture as a spiritual tool to enable abusers. The all-too-common refrain is, "God hates divorce, so stay and work out the problem because you made a vow for better or for worse." This hollow response merely beams a light on the inadequate education of ministers on how to counsel abused Black women.

Most pastors emphasize the notion that God is against divorce, advising abused women to stay and work on their marriages. This sort of counsel does nothing but send the wrong message. It insinuates that these women are to be blamed for the problem of abuse, and so it is their responsibility to fix it. According to Tracy Steven, "Clergy often tell abused women that they should be more submissive to their abusive husbands." This is a misguided generalization of the scripture, "the wife must be in submission to their own husbands as to the Lord" (Ephesians 5:22). These scriptures, many of which were written in a different era and social setting and which cannot rationally apply to today's world, are used as tools to enable abusive men. This misapplication of scripture is used by abusive men to justify their abusive behavior. Additionally, there is silence among the church leadership, and the church offers no help to these abused women who speak up. We should refuse to labor under any illusion. The church's silence regarding the abuse of women only serves to enable the abuser. It is now seemingly an established culture that African American women are expected to struggle in silence just to keep up with the appearance of a happy family. Sometimes, also, abused Black women suffer in silence because of shame. They often wonder, *What will the pastor think of me if I disclose the abuse by my husband? Will the church accept or reject me?* Often, women are vilified for speaking up, further enabling and prolonging psychological, physical, sexual, and financial oppression.

The history of the African American church as it relates to gender discrimination and the lackadaisical attitude of the Black church and its leadership is far from commendable. The Black church is under an obligation to seek to understand and address the dynamics of abusive relationships and issues of family violence. It is vital that the church acknowledges that domestic violence is a significant issue, and most certainly one that simply cannot be swept under the carpet. African American church leadership needs to acknowledge that Black women are being traumatized daily and that not a few of these abuses are being enabled and given tacit approval by church ministers. The stark truth is that it is only when the problem of domestic violence is acknowledged and then confronted headlong by church leadership that the work of healing can begin for abused Black women.

Gloria White-Hammond is copastor at Bethel American Methodist Episcopal Church in Boston. She writes, "The Black Church has a tremendous responsibility in combating domestic violence and sending the clear message that it is not acceptable." It is the inalienable responsibility of clergy and religious leaders to assume the leadership role in confronting and combating intimate partner violence. The reason for this is simple. The clergy is the vital key to unlocking the dynamics of domestic violence since abused women seek emotional support, godly counsel, and assistance from them. Without a doubt, every church is beset with its own peculiar set of internal conflicts and anomalies, and the African American church is no exception. Expectedly, there are differences in doctrinal conviction, gender discrimination issues, and cultural and diversity issues. However, when the church fails to adequately address these issues and disregards the fundamental rights of female church members, the result is that female members feel undervalued, and their collective self-worth suffers a grievous dent.

Domestic violence can only be accurately considered a horrifying abuse of a woman's right to live a life of freedom from assault and victimization. Leaving an intimate partner violence relationship can be, at the best of times, quite dangerous yet essential to the emotional, psychological, and physical well-being of an abused woman. The first and most critical action that must be taken when an abused woman approaches her church leadership for help is to ensure that she and her children are safe. It behooves the pastor to teach that all the members of the church community are to be their sister's keeper. Leaders should make a referral to a domestic violence shelter for DV counseling. For abused women to begin the healing process, pastoral care counselors ought to adopt a nonjudgmental attitude as they help to facilitate a safe environment for such hurting women and their children. In conclusion, the vital need for professional training for all church leaders, pastors, bishops, and ministers, simply cannot be overemphasized.

CHAPTER 12

The Effects of Pastoral Inadequacy

More men and women of God must learn and then
speak, preach and teach the truth about domestic
violence, how widespread it is and how some
Christian teachings can be twisted to condone, deny
and exacerbate it. Society and the church minimize
abuse. We must speak the truth and work together
to end domestic violence and sexual assault.
—Reverend Al Miles, lead chaplain,
the Queen's Medical Center, Honolulu, Hawaii,
author, *Domestic Violence: What
Every Pastor Needs to Know*

Family violence has become so commonplace and pervasive that it has assumed a horrifying normality in society today. People discuss the subject with a casualness akin to discussing the family menu for the week. Worse, the clergy, which ought to pour oil on troubled waters, has seemingly, and in a most cavalier manner, abandoned all attempts at viewing domestic violence with the seriousness it deserves, especially concerning the trauma to which the female members of their congregations are exposed on a daily basis. The worst of it all is that they have wittingly or unwittingly become complicit in the convenient triangulation that men indulge in while concealing their acts of domestic abuse and villainy. The tragedy of the entire affair is that some of the so-called pastors are themselves the worst offenders in the world of domestic violence.

That there is now a compelling need for educational workshops for members of the clergy on the dynamics of domestic violence is not in doubt. The late New Testament scholar Catherine Clark Kroeger traveled the globe opposing violence and the abuse of women while also advancing the biblical basis for the shared leadership and authority of men and women. Her most defining legacy is her wise leadership in the early evangelical women's movement of the 1970s. She also took a firm stand on the centrality of Scripture in responding to contemporary questions of gender and justice, in the process demonstrating uncommon compassion for abused women. According to research conducted with clergy by Kroeger and Nason-Clark, there were no universal or reliable practices in counseling abused wives.

There has always been a need for developing standards and practices for counseling women who are victims of domestic violence. Such intervention ought to be critically geared toward helping an abused woman move from being a victim to taking control of her life and relationship. First, the woman is helped to understand if her positive personality traits, such as hopefulness and deep empathy, have resulted in her missing potential warning signs, otherwise called *red flags*, in an abusive relationship. Then there is the need to determine whether the man abusing the woman has features of a personality disorder. Such individuals are often abusive because of their unhealthy beliefs and attitudes toward others. If this is the case, then the woman needs to let go of the hope that she can change her abuser as well as the guilt she may be carrying for the relationship not working.

Other unhealthy past relationships are explored, including those with her parents or other family members, which may have predisposed her to tolerate abusive behavior. The next stage includes educating the woman about practical strategies of assertiveness to deal with the abusers in her life. In this ideal scenario of proper counseling, a minister is expected to offer the compassion of a genuinely listening ear and provide scriptural validation for the woman's courage. Her pastor is supposed to help her understand that even though she has not received the love she had hoped for, she is still a beloved and worthwhile child of God. At this point, she is then able to decide whether to stay in the abusive relationship or leave it, rather than the pastor haranguing her with a "for better or for worse" pontification. In either case, the ultimate goal is for her to take back control of her life, deal assertively with the man who is abusing her, learn how to choose healthy partners, and become a healthy person herself.

Based on the findings of the Kroeger and Nason-Clark study, one can safely infer that there is a need for church leadership to adopt guidelines and consistent strategies on how to appropriately advise abused women. Research has alluded to a lack of sensitivity on the part of the church in the realm of counseling abused women, resulting in the breakdown of cohesion and inclusion within church communities and increasing the despairing sense of isolation among many Black church women, both within the church community and within their nuclear and extended family settings. On the other hand, the Kroeger and Nason-Clark study emphasizes that most members of the clergy are ill-equipped to counsel victims of family violence, with pastors commonly, and perhaps helplessly, making the recommendation that abused women stay and work on their marriages. More often than not, pastors advocate for and encourage abused wives to "save their marriage at any cost with quick-fix solutions for abusive men and abused women."

Of all the social problems confronted by the church, domestic violence is one of the most misunderstood and mismanaged by church leaders. Indeed, a high percentage of women do not view clergy as a source of help when they are victims of domestic violence.

Clergy often tells abused women that they should be more submissive to their abusive husbands. Some pastors simply say that abused wives should stay and trust God. Such pastors teach that the Bible unequivocally teaches wives to submit, even to abusive husbands. Sadly, submission does not stop abuse. In fact, it often serves to intensify the abuse, because it gives an abusive husband a greater sense of power and helps him circumvent painful consequences for his evil behavior.

Clergy rarely condemns domestic violence from the pulpit. While some clergy say very incorrect and harmful things in response to abuse, they are often silent about what *actually* needs to be said, namely, that God hates abuse and that domestic violence is sinful and unacceptable. This message is not only urgent for entire congregations, but it can be particularly empowering for abuse victims. This failure to condemn physical abuse from the pulpit is particularly puzzling in the Black church, which fundamentally believes that the Bible is the trustworthy word of God and that God intends it to guide and govern all of life. The condemnation of physical abuse is a dominant theme of Scripture, particularly in the Hebrew prophets. There are hundreds of Scripture passages that condemn abuse and proclaim God's particular judgment on physical abusers. For instance, one of the sins God hates is "hands that shed innocent blood" (Proverbs 6:17 NIV). The psalmist declares hatred of abuse by noting God's posture on physical abusers, "those who love violence his soul hates" (Psalm 11:5).

Clergy often minimizes the prevalence and gravity of domestic violence. Pastors consistently underestimate its prevalence in their own congregations. Not only do clergy often minimize the prevalence of domestic violence, but they also often minimize its gravity. This is particularly true for male clergy, most of whom have no experiential understanding of the fear and helplessness that women feel from abusive male partners who are much more powerful physically and socially. Sadly, the average pastor would say, "All couples have their arguments. What's the big deal?" or, "Many women exaggerate about their husbands' anger." In fact, domestic violence is very damaging. The Surgeon General of the United States has reported that domestic violence accounts for more adult female emergency room visits than traffic accidents, muggings, and rapes combined and is the greatest single cause of injury to American women. The US Department of Justice reports that approximately one-third of murdered women are killed by an intimate partner, and most victims of intimate partner homicide are killed by their husbands. Indeed, domestic violence is prevalent, and it is extremely damaging.

Clergy are often so concerned about preserving marriage that they advise against separation, let alone divorce from an abusive husband. This is largely the result of their being naive regarding the challenge of getting abusive men to change their behavior. A pastor once told an abused woman, "You are responsible for mollifying your husband. You have to be perfect in your behavior toward him, and you must be very sensitive to avoid anything that will set him off." The average pastor places the guilt on the abused woman's shoulders. She is blamed for not submitting to her husband. Abusive husbands hardly ever change after so-called pastoral counseling. In fact, they often become more abusive than ever. The stark truth is that, ultimately, abusive men do not abuse because of what their wives do or do not do. They abuse because of complex internal pathologies that are beyond the wife's control or responsibility.

While pastors often fail to adequately help victims of domestic violence, it must be recognized that they have tremendous power to encourage and help victims heal. As they become educated regarding the dynamics of domestic violence, the damage to victims, and the patterns of violence exhibited by abusers, they will be able to offer wise counsel and assistance. The most important things pastors can do are to listen humbly to these women, truly hear what they have experienced, and ask what they need from the church. Such a response is essential because pastors who have not experienced abuse will not intuitively recognize the needs of abused women. Furthermore, since such women have been systematically devalued, demeaned, and stripped of power, it can be very affirming for pastors to humbly seek out the needs of abused women. Humility is critical here since abuse victims have very fragile egos and tend to be filled with shame.

Sometimes, pastors are in deep denial when one of their members is charged with abuse since the abuser seemed like such a nice person and did not look like anyone who could abuse. In fact, abusers cannot be visually identified, but they do have some notable behavioral characteristics. The first and most consistent characteristic of abusive men is a pervasive denial of responsibility. They simply refuse to own their destructive behavior. They do this by shifting the blame for their abuse or by minimizing the abuse itself.

Rare is the abuser who condones abuse in general. They say that abuse is wrong, but what they did was not abuse. Alternatively, they might say that their wives forced them into violence by being such a nag, disrespecting their authority, or not meeting their sexual needs. Pervasive denial of responsibility is exactly what we see in the life of King Saul, whose heart so displeased God that God rejected him from being king. The education of pastors should teach them to start asking such questions like the following:

- What are some of the most common effects of domestic violence on wives and children?
- What specifically does Scripture have to say about physical abuse?
- What does the healing process look like for survivors of domestic violence?
- What do abusive men need from the church?
- Once an abusive man says he is sorry and wants to change, what would real repentance and change look like?

Also, pastors should condemn abuse from the pulpit and broadly educate the congregation on abuse. This is one of the most significant ways that clergy can encourage abuse victims and create a climate for healing. It is very empowering and encouraging for abused women to hear their ministers declare from the pulpit, "God hates abuse," "God promises to judge harshly all unrepentant physical abusers," or "There can never be any excuse for touching your girlfriend or wife in anger." These statements are solidly biblical and need to be proclaimed from the pulpit.

Churches also need education on various aspects of domestic violence, including what constitutes domestic violence, the signs of domestic violence, characteristics of abusers, the nature of dating violence, God's perspective on violence, what Scripture teaches about gender equality, the dignity of women, and how believers can respond to domestic violence. This education can occur in various church settings, including Sunday sermons, premarital counseling, women's ministry events, men's discipleship groups, and youth groups.

It is important for pastors to prioritize the protection of abuse victims and their children. That means pastors must take seriously all reports of domestic violence, must never minimize abuse victims' concerns, and must be willing to confront abusers boldly and offer practical assistance to victims. This includes helping victims of domestic violence develop a safety plan and access safe housing, and assisting them with financial needs. That prioritization also includes encouraging and supporting women to separate from abusive husbands. Abusive husbands cause tremendous long-term physical, emotional, and spiritual damage to children, even if they only physically abuse the mother. Meanwhile, it must be noted that roughly half of men who physically abuse their wives also abuse their children. We also know that the most common factor among men who abuse their wives is that they experienced domestic violence themselves in childhood. Additionally, we know that girls who grow up in physically abusive homes are several times more likely to be physically and sexually victimized in adulthood due to the emotional damage of childhood abuse, or even simply witnessing it. All of this shows that growing up in a physically abusive home, whether or not one is actually beaten, is extremely damaging in the long-term and certainly "causes the little ones to stumble."

Separation from an abusive husband is also ethically important for the well-being of the woman because domestic violence creates serious physical, emotional, and spiritual damage. Scripture most certainly does not commend enduring avoidable suffering. Pastors should advise abused wives to flee from their abusive husbands and should assist them in every way they can to find safety and physical security.

Conclusively, pastors have generally failed to adequately and helpfully respond to domestic violence, but this can change. They have a tremendous influence on healing and protection. If they are well-educated on the dynamics of domestic violence and develop the courage to condemn domestic violence from the pulpit, the cycle of violence will be broken, and the Body of Christ can become a place of safety and divine healing.

CHAPTER 13

For the Love and the Liberation of Woman

When we denigrate a woman, we are in fact diminishing part of the image of God. When we exclude women, we exclude part of God. When we put women down, we tarnish the image of God.

—Christine Caine

There is no doubt that Jesus was fundamentally opposed to the religious traditions and cultural practices of the era in which He pursued His ministry. That was because those religious traditions and cultural practices were rigged in favor of men and totally oppressive to women. The Jewish elite of the day were afflicted by an unbridled lust for power, unleashing unheard-of restrictions that were not only unjust but also patently inhumane to women. To mitigate their reign of terror on women, Jesus made His timely appearance as the long-awaited Messiah. Jesus came to demonstrate the heart of the Creator—a heart of *love* and *liberation*. That love was unshackled by any type of condition and became classically known as unconditional love, while the liberation was actually *liberation from all forms of oppression*.

In His infinite wisdom, Jesus was fully cognizant of the innate worth of women, and He demonstrated that acknowledgment in the way He addressed women. Jesus always spoke to them in a kind, caring, and tender manner. When He addressed the woman who had suffered a flow of blood for twelve years, He called her daughter. He said to her, "Daughter, your faith has healed you. Go in peace and be freed from your suffering" (Mark 5:34). Similarly, He referred to the bent woman as a "daughter of Abraham." He said, "Then should not this woman, a daughter of Abraham, whom Satan has kept bound for eighteen long years, be set free on the Sabbath day from what bound her?" (Luke 13:16). In what might be accurately construed as an attempt to bring liberation to all women, Jesus spoke with love and empathy to any woman with whom He came in contact.

At dawn one morning, Jesus went to the temple to teach. The people gathered around, ready to be taught. The Pharisees suddenly rushed up to Him. They had a woman with them. "Teacher, this woman was caught in the act of adultery," they said (John 8:4).

We can only begin to imagine this woman's plight. She must have been dragged humiliatingly through the streets under the stares of her neighbors. Clearly, there would be no erasing the damage now done to her reputation. From that day, she would be the subject of whispers and malicious gossip. She had, after all, been seemingly caught in the act. She had violated the law. We don't even know the unknown details. Had she been seduced, perhaps even pressured or forced, by an unscrupulous man? Did she give in, in a moment of weakness? The Bible is silent on the details. Yet those details are not the point of the story, but rather Jesus's response to her when her shameful adultery was publicly exposed.

Meanwhile, only the woman was brought before Jesus. Apparently, only the hapless woman was considered enough of an offender to be brought to the temple for immediate judgment. The man was spared judgment. For a woman, adultery was not just a cause of deep shame but also potentially a capital offense.

The Pharisees challenged Jesus, "In the law, Moses commanded us to stone such women. Now what do you say?" (John 8:5).

This wasn't merely a matter of wanting to adhere to the purest interpretation of justice according to the law. They were using this question as a trap in order to have a basis for accusing Jesus.

This woman was their bait. Would Jesus give a nod to stoning her or disregard the law? Jesus didn't take the bait. He cleverly distracted the attention of the crowd from the humiliated woman. He knelt and wrote on the ground with His finger. The Pharisees looked at each other, confused, and remained silent for a few moments to see whether He would speak. When He didn't, they began assaulting Him with questions again. Eventually, He stood up and spoke. "Let any one of you who is without sin be the first to throw a stone at her" (John 8:7).

Then He knelt and wrote on the ground again. In a gesture of mercy toward the woman, Jesus once again drew all eyes away from her and toward Himself as He knelt. All eyes were on Jesus as He made a show of writing on the ground. He had interceded for her already. Yet He hadn't said a word to her yet. He had taken all her shame and humiliation on Himself and given her a respite. As if this weren't sufficient relief, what happened next was equally astonishing. The crowd began to drift away, the older ones first. Jesus didn't stand until the crowd had dispersed. Then He turned to the woman and said, "Woman, where are they? Has no one condemned you?" (John 8:10).

"No one, sir," the woman replied.

"Then neither do I condemn you. Go now and leave your life of sin" (John 8:11).

One could argue that the woman was brought for judgment because of her sin, but that would be only partly true. If justice had been the real goal, then the man would have been charged as well. *Actually, this woman was guilty of the crime of being a woman caught in adultery.* Women in that culture were second-class citizens at best, akin to slaves. Men had complete authority over their wives and daughters and made all decisions regarding relationships and activities. Part of Jewish law taught that women were like Gentile slaves and could be obtained by intercourse, money, or written contract. Women had few rights inside the home and practically none outside of it. They were not counted as members during a synagogue count and received little or no religious education, except from their husbands if he so desired. Men were discouraged from speaking to women on the street. It was clearly a male-dominated society.

The history of our world is rampant with oppression, diminishment, contempt, and hostility aimed at women. Even today, women are stoned to death for adultery in India and Pakistan. They are raped and sold as slaves in Syria. The men who perpetrate these horrendous acts are excused with religious theology. In every case, in every century, women have been targets.

Of all places on earth, the Christian church could and should be the most significant place of healing and hope. The Church is supposed to be the place where women can experience the joys of being respected, appreciated, esteemed, included, and celebrated. After all, God Himself made women in His image. He created male and female. God's image is only fully reflected in both man and woman. Christine Caine, Australian evangelist and activist, wrote, "When we denigrate a woman, we are in fact diminishing part of the image of God. When we exclude women, we exclude part of God. When we put women down, we tarnish the image of God." Male and female are equally loved and valued by God. Paul wrote to the Galatians stating this very point, "There is neither Jew nor Gentile, neither slave nor free, nor is there male and female, for you are all one in Christ Jesus" (Galatians 3:28). In Christ, there is no distinction in value between male and female. No one dignifies, affirms, and celebrates women like the God of the Bible. Therefore, it should be the church that leads the way and sets the example of placing value upon womanhood and of getting them to Jesus, who can lift their shame and totally liberate them.

Indeed, the world that Jesus was born into largely marginalized women. Despite that, Jesus treated women as equal to men. Jesus's countercultural regard for women was nothing short of remarkable for His day. Yet Jesus's extraordinary treatment of women and His esteem for women is rooted in God's esteem for women. Throughout history, God has made His respect for women clear in bold ways.

Starting in Genesis, we read that God declared that He created mankind in His own image, "male and female He created them." God's profound respect for women was also front and center when He sent His angel Gabriel to the virgin who would bear God's only Son without the involvement of a man in the conception. After Jesus's birth, God continued to emphasize the integral role of women. We see one example during Jesus's consecration at the Temple of Jerusalem, where Mary and Joseph encountered Anna, a prophet and elderly widow. Upon seeing the infant Jesus, Anna began praising God and speaking of Jesus "to all who were looking forward to the redemption of Jerusalem." As an elderly widow, Anna would have been one of the lowest-regarded members of society in biblical times. Despite this, God gave Anna the authority to proclaim His will as a prophet. God further blessed Anna by giving her the special knowledge to recognize Jesus as our Savior while He was still an infant.

Then at the end of Jesus's earthly life, God continued to exalt the role of women. We see this in the fact that God chose a woman, Mary Magdalene, to be the first witness to the most significant event in all of Christianity, the resurrection of Jesus Christ.

Given society's misogynistic sentiments toward women in Jesus's day, Jesus's interactions with women were shocking to onlookers and revolutionary in hindsight. At a time when society regarded women as something to be disregarded at will, Jesus reminded His fellow Jews that God created women in His image in the same way that He created men in His image. "'Haven't you read,' He replied, 'that at the beginning the Creator "made them male and female"'" (Matthew 19:4).

At a time when others regarded women as unworthy company, Jesus kept close ties with Mary, Martha, and Mary Magdalene. Jesus even kept company with women who had been possessed and disease-ridden. This included Mary Magdalene, who had been cleansed of seven demons. When others saw women as inferior intellectually, Jesus preached to Mary at His feet, the typical place for a male disciple to sit. Jesus didn't object to Mary's desire to learn and didn't question her capacity to understand what He taught. Instead, He commended Mary for making the better choice of hearing the Teacher speak, asserting, "But few things are needed, or indeed only one. Mary has chosen what is better, and it will not be taken away from her" (Luke 10:42).

In continuing to reject cultural norms, the longest conversation Jesus had with an individual in the New Testament was with a woman—a Samaritan woman He encountered at Jacob's well. For a man to address a woman in public was scandalous at the time. Importantly, this Samaritan woman was also the first person to whom Jesus revealed that He was the long-awaited Messiah. This woman went on to become a missionary for Jesus, bringing others in her town to Christ. In continuing to make groundbreaking revelations specifically to women, the Resurrected Christ not only appeared first to Mary Magdalene, but He also commissioned her to be the first to give testimony of His Resurrection. This fact is especially radical when you consider that women in biblical times were seen as unreliable witnesses at best and were not allowed to testify in court.

Jesus's esteem for the plight of women is seen elsewhere in Scripture. At Jesus's crucifixion, His mother Mary is presumed to have been a widow. With rare exceptions, widows in ancient Israel suffered a sort of cultural death by being relegated to the fringes of society and usually ending up in extreme poverty. As a widow, Mary may have been headed for a similar fate. However, Jesus kept His mother's well-being in mind despite the excruciating pain He endured at His crucifixion. Scripture tells us that as He hung, Christ entrusted the apostle John with Mary's care.

We also see Jesus's concern for the plight of disregarded women when He cured a woman who had been crippled for eighteen years on the Sabbath. When the synagogue leader confronted Jesus for having healed the woman on the Sabbath, Jesus defiantly declared the woman a *daughter of Abraham*. "Then should not this woman, a daughter of Abraham, whom Satan has kept bound for eighteen long years, be set free on the Sabbath day from what bound her?" (Luke 13:16). In making this bold assertion, Jesus put her, and all other women, on par in Jewish society with their male counterparts, or the "sons of Abraham."

The Jewish law in Jesus's time had many rules as to what was considered ritually unclean. A woman was considered to be unclean if she was menstruating. As such, anyone or anything that touched her during this time was also deemed ritually impure. Jesus, however, refused to treat women as unclean. This is dramatically played out in the Bible's account of the woman who had been bleeding for twelve years. Here, Jesus was making His way through a crowd toward an official's house to heal the official's sick daughter when the woman with the menstrual disorder touched Jesus's cloak. Such an action made Jesus unclean according to Jewish law. Just then, Jesus stopped walking toward the official's house and insisted that the person who had touched Him step forward from the crowd. When the trembling woman came forward and explained her actions, Jesus did not furiously admonish her for her risky, ritually impure action. Instead, Jesus called the woman "daughter" and commended her for putting faith before man-made law. Jesus viewed women as being just as capable as men, possessing the power to make sound judgments and self-determination. Jesus clearly viewed women not as objects, but as individuals created in the image of God. Jesus chose many women to exemplify His teaching. He showed consideration to women and believed that they should be permitted a place at the table for the teaching of the Scriptures. Jesus raised the bar of gender equality, as there was no gender discrimination in learning from Jesus.

James Cone was a Methodist minister and theologian best known for his advocacy of black liberation theology. He asked the question, "What does Jesus have to do with all of this? All this oppression?" In his book *God of the Oppressed*, Cone argues that Christ is on the side of the oppressed, not the oppressors. Therefore, the true story of Jesus cannot be understood from the perspective of the dominant in society. Cone argues that the story of Jesus is only true when it is understood as the story of God's *liberation of oppressed people*. In Cone's conviction, there is a strong connection of liberation embedded in the history of slavery and the oppression of Black people. Without a doubt, the gospel is hope in Jesus, the great liberator and redeemer. There is hope for women who continue to experience emotional and physical abuse and discrimination in a male-dominant society. Jesus came to liberate all those who are oppressed. God identifies with all those who are oppressed and mistreated. In the times of our suffering, God is there with every weeping and broken woman.

The bigger question is, why does a good God allow innocent people to be victimized by those who misuse their power? Scripture gives every woman experiencing abuse the assurance and promise that no matter what the oppression, and no matter what emotional pain they may be suffering, God will send deliverance in due season. Tricia Bent-Goodley is a mental health clinician and a professor at Howard University. She wrote, "African American women are at elevated risk for nonfatal and lethal intimate partner violence." Women who have experienced abuse also experience psychological trauma, which has short- and long-term consequences. An abusive relationship involves physical suffering and psychological pain that can have long-lasting implications. Bent-Goodley states that domestic violence affects more than five million Americans each year, more than 85 percent of whom are women. Many of these women turn to their faith-based communities for support and guidance, but little is known about how church leadership or church members in general understand or perceive domestic violence. James Cone would further write, "Liberation theology teaches that God wants everyone to be free and that God promises victory over the destructive forces of the world that oppose this freedom."

For victims who have endured actual threats of death, verbal deprecation, and physical assault resulting in serious injury, there is a need for safety plans, intervention, and freedom from abuse. For women going through domestic violence, Jesus says, "Woman, you are set free from your infirmity" (Luke 13:12). Jesus is still announcing, "Woman, you are liberated! I have come to set you free!" The meaning of the word *freedom* is *deliverance*—to advance to a higher state of being. To be free means to be exempt from the power and control of another individual. The message of the gospel is one of *hope*, *liberation*, and *restoration* for all people. Love came in the person of Jesus Christ to bring freedom to abused women—women under the yoke of cultural injustice, religious bondage, and oppression.

CHAPTER 14

The Family as Victim

Children are seriously harmed by observing the
controlling and demeaning behaviors and words shown
toward a parent. Such parental behaviors result in severe
stress in the home which damages a child's happiness,
hopefulness, trust and confidence even if the child is
not the recipient of these words and behaviors. The
emotional pain in these children, which includes a great
deal of anger, is often unconscious... Subsequently,
many of these children develop cognitive difficulties.

—Richard P. Fitzgibbons

The home is supposed to be a safe space in which to grow up, develop, and thrive. In any case, it is only to be expected that we will rely on those closest to us for guidance and support as we trudge our way through the early developmental stages of life. That is why, as soon as our home transforms into a tumultuous setting for violence, the stage is set for severe and wide-ranging effects across the entire family.

Domestic violence, which, as we now know, is defined as violent behavior on the part of an intimate partner, can lead to serious mental and physical effects, some of which may not even be readily apparent. In the context of this discussion on the effects of domestic violence on the family, I will take the pains to remind us of what domestic violence, more specifically termed intimate partner violence, entails in a romantic relationship or a marriage. It invariably involves the physical, sexual, emotional, or financial abuse of one person by another. In the family setting, common forms of abuse can include unwanted or unsolicited physical contact, ranging from the occasional aggressive shove to sexual assault or rape, emotional manipulation, accusations of infidelity, threats of harm, and the assertion of control through denial of financial support or other resources.

Usually, the abuser is the physically stronger person in the relationship and, through violence, will often use this strength to exert control over the abused. In the family setting, women and children are generally the most common victims of domestic violence. Surprisingly, many people do not even recognize domestic violence for what it is. When you don't know what signs to look for, it can be difficult to recognize abuse. Indeed, many victims don't immediately know that they are experiencing domestic violence. Many even believe that, at the time of the abuse, it is merely a one-time occurrence. Yet the more tragic reality is that domestic violence almost invariably develops into a pattern of behavior that worsens over time.

We now recognize that domestic violence affects people from all backgrounds, races, and classes. Recent statistics from the US Centers for Disease Control (CDC) suggest that domestic violence is a reality for approximately 41 percent of women in the United States. Equally disturbing is the fact that one out of every seven children in the United States will experience abuse or neglect. Despite the fact that domestic violence is so widespread, it often goes unreported, rendering its true prevalence somewhat a mystery. Many women who experience abuse do not report it for various reasons, including fear of retaliation, shame, and concern regarding the response of others. Among Black women, there is an unfortunate lack of appropriate response from the leaders of their church, which ordinarily might be considered their safest haven for safety and security.

People respond to traumatic events in different ways. That means the effects of domestic abuse will vary from person to person. Yet understanding the general effects of abuse can create a more empathetic and supportive societal experience for victims of abuse.

Women who experience domestic violence can develop post-traumatic stress disorder (PTSD). In fact, research shows that women who experience intimate partner violence statistically develop PTSD at a rate of between 51 percent and 75 percent, which is well above the approximately 10 percent rate experienced by the general population of women. Other mental health concerns that can develop in an abusive setting include depression, anxiety disorders, and substance use disorder. Additionally, an abused woman may feel that she has lost control. In some cases, such women even start to believe that they deserve the abuse they are suffering at the hands of their partners, and this ultimately leads to a struggle with self-esteem. The physical effects of abuse can be devastating and might include bruising, fractured bones, tension, disruptions in dietary or sleep patterns, and exhaustion. In the home and outside the home, women try to cover up these signs of abuse with long clothing or makeup, so as not to draw attention from other members of society. Additionally, women who are experiencing abuse might exhibit uncharacteristic behavior. For example, a woman who is known to be a generally happy and energetic person may suddenly become withdrawn and reserved.

The foregoing is all about the abused woman. *What about her children?* This is where matters take a turn for the singularly pathetic. Even if a child is not directly abused, when they grow up in an environment of domestic abuse or violence, they tend to live with fear and intense feelings of sadness. This can lead to the formation of mental health conditions later on, such as depression and substance use disorder. A child growing up in an abusive environment may also struggle with preparing for the future, possibly leading to challenges at school and behavioral anomalies. Children may also internalize the negative effects of abuse. What complicates matters for even the most observant is that the effects of domestic violence are not always readily evident. Most children experiencing domestic violence will try to hide it. However, signs to watch out for can include low self-esteem, nightmares, apathy, regression and withdrawal, lack of concentration, sleep difficulties, bedwetting, and stuttering. When children in an abusive setting transition to the adolescent stage, they may exhibit such symptoms as poor school grades, absences from school, or dropping out of school entirely. Others will include eating disorders, depression, and substance use disorder, and they may even become abusive themselves, either to their peers or to their parents. Sometimes, they may run away from home or look for excuses not to go home. Such adolescents may entertain suicidal thoughts, engage in risky behavior, get entangled in law enforcement issues, have trouble making or keeping friends, and, overall, wallow in feelings of extreme low self-esteem.

In the average family abuse setting, the severity of a child's symptoms can increase over time and might depend on the length of time the child has been exposed to abuse, the extent of the abuse, and the age of the child. Overall, however, domestic violence can have far-reaching impacts on family members who witness it. It can negatively affect one's physical and mental health, as well as their ability to function and embrace life. Ultimately, children deserve to have a safe, nurturing home life and to experience the mental and emotional well-being that often accompanies it. Sadly, domestic violence is a harrowing reality that now affects countless families. Beyond the immediate physical and emotional harm inflicted on the direct victim, domestic abuse has far-reaching consequences that extend to the entire family unit.

The family is a very real victim of domestic violence. Domestic abuse creates an atmosphere of fear, tension, and instability within the family. Witnessing or experiencing abuse can lead to severe emotional trauma and lasting psychological effects on all family members, especially children. The constant exposure to abuse can result in anxiety, depression, post-traumatic stress disorder (PTSD), low self-esteem, and a sense of helplessness. The emotional scars inflicted by domestic abuse may persist long after the abuse has ended, impacting the overall well-being and functioning of family members.

Worse, domestic abuse erodes trust within the family unit. The abused woman will definitely struggle to trust her abuser, leading to a breakdown of their intimate relationship. Additionally, children growing up in an environment marred by violence will have difficulty trusting others and forming healthy relationships in the future. The cycle of abuse can disrupt the bonds between family members, creating a sense of isolation, resentment, and strained communication.

Children exposed to domestic abuse are particularly vulnerable to long-lasting consequences. Witnessing abuse can result in long-lasting emotional and behavioral problems, such as aggression, withdrawal, academic difficulties, and challenges with forging healthy attachments. With such children growing up in an environment of chronic stress and instability, it is hardly surprising that their emotional development is hindered, and this leads to challenges with social interactions and educational attainment. Naturally, domestic abuse also affects the dynamics of parenting. An abused woman will struggle with her parenting role due to the emotional toll the abuse is taking on her. Additionally, her abuser might be using manipulation and control tactics to undermine the woman's authority. Ultimately, the overall parenting environment becomes compromised, impacting the children's emotional security and overall well-being.

Not surprisingly, families experiencing domestic abuse often face social isolation and stigma. Shame and the fear of judgment often constrain them from seeking support or disclosing their situation to others. Commonly, an abusive husband will isolate his victim from friends and family, aiming to create a sense of dependency since alternative sources of support have been cut off. The abused Black woman enters a vicious cycle in which the lack of a strong social network exacerbates feelings of helplessness, making it challenging for the family to break free from the cycle of abuse.

In talking about cycles, we must not fail to acknowledge one of the most devastating consequences of domestic abuse on families: the perpetuation of what is seemingly an *intergenerational cycle of abuse*. Children who witness or experience abuse are at higher risk of becoming either victims or perpetrators of abuse in their own relationships as adults. Without intervention and support, the damaging patterns established by domestic abuse can continue from one generation to the next, perpetuating a cycle that affects the overall well-being of individuals, families, and entire communities.

The family is also a victim in terms of the severe economic consequences it often has to endure in times of domestic strife. Women often face obstacles in securing and maintaining employment due to the physical and emotional effects of abuse. Economic control tactics employed by an abusive husband, such as restricting access to financial resources, can further exacerbate financial instability. Families may experience financial hardship, limited access to resources, and challenges in meeting basic needs, adding additional layers of stress and vulnerability.

As I already mentioned, children growing up in an environment of domestic abuse often face educational challenges. The chronic stress and emotional turmoil they experience tend to impede their ability to focus and concentrate on their studies. The instability occasioned by domestic turmoil often leads to frequent school changes, absences, or difficulties in forming relationships with peers and teachers. Naturally, these educational implications tend to have long-term consequences on their educational attainment and future opportunities. Of far greater social implication is the fact that the consequences of domestic abuse extend beyond the immediate family context. It affects an individual's future relationships. Both victims and witnesses of abuse may struggle with establishing healthy and trusting relationships. The trauma and negative experiences associated with domestic abuse can shape their beliefs, behaviors, and expectations, making it challenging to engage in relationships built on mutual respect, trust, and equality.

Ultimately, the family structure is disrupted, with the abusive dynamics often leading to separation, divorce, or a woman's decision to leave the relationship for a safer and more secure environment. Such decisions can have profound implications for the entire family, including changes in living arrangements, financial strain, and the need for legal intervention, such as battles for the custody of the children. The disruption of the family structure further compounds the challenges faced by family members and can have a lasting impact on their sense of stability and security.

With a more than 50 percent divorce rate in the United States today, most people can recall what it was like to feel like pawns in a parental war. Naturally, by the time divorce becomes a rational option, there are many angry, resentful, and bitter feelings accumulated during the course of the marital relationship. Very few divorces are friendly and amicable. In fact, more often than not, an abusive husband will be all too willing to display his vindictiveness by using the children as weapons in the divorce war. Naturally, the only victims of this type of behavior are the children. In many cases, the abuser wages a bitter custody battle against his children's mother in an attempt to obtain sole custody of the children while severely restricting the visiting rights of their mother. The motivation for this act of vindictiveness is simply to exact revenge against the victim of abuse for the perceived audacity she had in seeking to terminate the abusive marriage.

The consequences of divorce can be devastating for children. Children identify with each of their parents. If they end up perceiving one parent as evil, which they will perceive their abusive father as, they will come to believe that this is true of them as well. *How can it not be so? If my father is a bad person, it must mean I am a bad person too.* Naturally, also, it is common for children to misunderstand what is happening between their parents and to blame themselves for the situation. They are also quick to believe that one or both parents are leaving home because he, the child, is not loved. In some cases, a child who witnesses a parent packing and moving may fear that he, the child, will be told to leave home forever. Young children, with fragile emotions and dependent upon nurturing and love, may pretend that they do not care that one parent has left and throw themselves even more upon the parent who is present. For the child who experiences the loss of a parent, because that parent has been successfully blocked from participation in the child's life, the consequences are even worse. Many studies show that divorce can result in children growing into adults who have much lower self-esteem compared to those who were raised by both parents. Quite frankly, divorce is difficult enough for everyone without embroiling the children in the angry politics of the adults.

In conclusion, domestic violence inflicts devastating consequences on families, affecting every aspect of their lives. From emotional trauma and psychological effects to the breakdown of trust and relationships, the impact of domestic abuse on families is quite profound. In totality, it affects the development of children, the dynamics of parenting, interactions with the larger society, and economic stability. Also, the intergenerational cycle of abuse does nothing but perpetuate the harmful patterns, while the health and well-being of family members suffer immensely.

The main purpose for my writing exhaustively on the subject of domestic abuse is to raise awareness of the impact of domestic abuse on families and to advocate for support systems that address the needs of both victims and their children. By promoting prevention, early intervention, and comprehensive support services, we can work toward breaking the cycle of abuse and creating a society that values healthy, safe, and nurturing family relationships. Together, we can support those affected by domestic abuse and pave the way for the process of therapeutic healing, resilience, the empowerment of abused women, and a brighter future for families, faith communities, and the entire society.

CHAPTER 15

Surviving Intimate Partner Violence

You can write me down in history with
hateful, twisted lies, you can tread me in this
very dirt, but still, like dust, I will rise.
—Maya Angelou, poet and educator

Most abused women continue to work through the fall-out long after they leave their traumatic relationship. For those who are fortunate enough to immediately go into intensive trauma therapy, instant help comes to process all that they had to endure. However, as has been unequivocally proven, perhaps the most important work someone leaving an abusive relationship can do is to try to heal through emerging personal relationships. This is vital because it provides the opportunity to relearn how to trust, how to beneficially collaborate, and how to, once more, grow with others. This sort of healing process also serves the purpose of reminding one that safety and comfort are still possible and that anyone who genuinely cares will be gentle and patient.

Healing through new relationships is often the hardest work for survivors of intimate partner violence because trauma will invariably cause victims to feel distant from and untrusting of others. It will also cause them to avoid intimacy. Sahana Prasad, a Michigan-based trauma therapist, says, "Lots of survivors ask questions about how to know if something's really a red flag or if their trauma brain is being triggered, and the only good answer to that question is practice. We have to learn those relational skills in a safe and supportive environment. We heal through relationships, even if our trauma tells us we have to isolate."

It is certainly not uncommon to find that many survivors have had multiple abusive relationships. This is not necessarily because they, wittingly or unwittingly, attract abusers or because they are "bad" at building and nurturing healthy relationships or any of the other myths that have been perpetuated about failed relationships. Sahana Prasad further says, "It's important for survivors to remember that if you've been in more than one violent or abusive relationship, it's not your fault. There is a significant part of your brain that consciously or subconsciously may be trying to make sense of what has happened to you by gravitating toward similar people who you want to have different dynamics or endings with, and the way to break that pattern is to recognize that it is happening and to seek support from people in your life who can see those types of patterns from the outside."

Survivors cannot heal alone. They need other people: family, friends, pastoral care counselors, mental health professionals, and DV counselors, to help them examine and reconcile with their patterns and support them through their self-exploration. They also need to have healthy relationships through which they can experience conflict and confusion and still be safe at the end of the day. Certain strategies can help, including setting boundaries, advocating for oneself, and asking for what one needs for a relationship to be genuinely beneficial.

Significantly, for me, I drew from my personal relationship with my Heavenly Father Almighty God (Yahweh) by increasing my engagement in spiritual practices, including time spent in prayer, finding the space for meditation and solitude. It is also important to realize that, as a survivor of abuse, one is not alone. Many abuse survivors experience the healing power of social connection by employing different relational practices. There is this commonly held notion that you have to learn to love yourself before you can love others. In fact, a lot of self-help literature might make you feel like you have to go and crawl into a hole and fix yourself all alone in that hole before you can even broach the idea of interacting with other people.

The popular saying is that "hurt people hurt people." The simple truth is that the only way you can learn to *trust* and *love* is to be in community with others. You need to learn how to ask for your needs to be met, and how to have healthy conflicts and resolve them. You simply cannot do all that by yourself.

In cultivating relationships to heal from abuse, it can be very helpful to take note of who is actively and enthusiastically committed to healthy communication. We all make mistakes, but who is willing to admit that and do better? It is crucial to cultivate relationships with people as committed to healing as you are. That commitment may look different depending on a person's own mental health struggles and journey. Therefore, patience is key with some people. Yet that shouldn't stop you from respectfully distancing yourself from those who are not interested in building safe, healthy, and secure relationships. It can be a useful act of self-preservation to limit such people's access to you.

Once you start getting to know new people better, you will feel confident in telling them more details of your abusive relationship. This will be helpful because you could then explain that you might need their support. It should come as no surprise if, for a long time, you find it difficult to trust people, believing that people will not support you. You will have to learn that you can actually ask for help and get it. After all, you don't just exist to be of benefit to others. You also exist to love and be loved; it is your God-given birthright.

For the average survivor of domestic violence, honesty and straightforwardness in communication are vital. It can be particularly jolting to get the impression someone isn't saying what they mean. Therefore, recognizing emotions and responding honestly is something you ought to hold your loved ones accountable for, and you should encourage them to do the same with you. Boundary setting is of absolutely vital importance. It is important that you set boundaries for things that might potentially cause you harm while also proactively setting expectations for how you might feel supported and cared for. In normal, healthy relationships, there is two-way open communication, and there doesn't need to be a pushback of any sort to actually be heard or have your needs met. Of equal importance, you shouldn't feel like you're constantly giving and giving when the other person just isn't considering your feelings.

It is important to remain open, flexible, and patient with yourself and with others. Whenever you are in a place where you are having a difficult time navigating interpersonal relationships because of your history of trauma, you need to start thinking about yourself and others with a certain compassion. You need to be kind to yourself and to others. We need to be kind to one another. We all have the responsibility to support those who are weak and struggling. We must be willing to turn inward and ask, "How can I be of service to those who are beaten, broken, and oppressed?" and, "How are my experiences of the past connecting to the present in ways that might help others?"

Think about relationships and community like a garden. Everything about our lives is interconnected and the environment in which we find ourselves. The support and care we both give and receive profoundly affect us. For example, as in gardening, the first year's yield of plants and flowers, in all likelihood, will not be perfect. In any case, there is never any such thing as a "perfect" yield. It takes many years to learn how to nurture different plants and flowers and to gain sufficient familiarity with what each of them needs. Some need more sun or less water or to be moved somewhere else entirely. Relationships, and the process of healing from abuse, bear a striking similarity to the existence of flowering plants in a garden. Sometimes we are the gardeners, and sometimes we are the plants and flowers that need tending to. When we blame ourselves for not cultivating healthy relationships and come down hard on ourselves simply because we haven't yet found the solutions we are looking for, we *shrink*. That is because we are not giving ourselves permission to learn what the flowering plants in the garden need for them to *bloom*. Yet nothing quite celebrates the beauty of life like a flower in full bloom. Nothing quite suggests a certain hope for the future like the life and energy in the colorful beauty of a flower. It is that life and energy that the survivor of abuse needs to navigate her way to a happier and more fulfilling life. Indeed, when we choose to be curious and investigate what we need from others, and what we can do for them in return, there are so many ways to grow and so many possibilities for a greater future ahead for us.

What can we do to change the church culture that domestic violence is a private matter? Pastors need to have a clear biblical understanding that Scriptures can be used as a means to further empower abusive men. Scriptures were written during a different time and social setting, and some do not apply to today's context. Consequently, the misuse of Scripture enables abusive men to minimize and justify their abusive behaviors. How can pastors bring about change in their local congregations? Church leaders are called to be caretakers of the Body of Christ. When women are told by pastors to work on their marriages, this counsel sends the wrong message because it implies that abused women are at fault for the problem of abuse; hence, it is their responsibility to fix it. If Scripture is to be accepted as God's Word and to be believed by all people, then there should be no tolerance for abuse or oppression of any kind in the privacy of Christian homes. The mutual love, respect, and harmony as ordained in the marriage relationship at Creation should be realized.

Ultimately, what is important is for a survivor of intimate partner violence to know that there is a bright future ahead. For such women, the questions often come up, "Why did you stay so long?" "Why didn't you just leave?" There are numerous reasons why she didn't just leave and why she remained in a relationship that could have killed her. To start with, there is *fear*. She had both a *fear of staying* and a *fear of leaving*. Statistics show that in a domestic abuse situation, if the abuser has access to a gun, it increases the chances that the woman will die by 500 percent. That is because the final step in the domestic violence pattern is to kill the abused.

Dear survivor of abuse, know one thing for sure. Domestic violence might have possessed the potential of seeing you die unhappy and unloved at the hands of your abuser. But God obviously had other plans for you. That is why you are alive and reading this book. Indeed, it is my hope that if, as you read this book, you are in the midst of a violent relationship or you know anyone who is, you can see that there is a way out. You must refuse to suffer alone simply because you believe that keeping silent appears safer than speaking out.

It takes a long time to forgive yourself, especially if you tend to be hard on yourself. You probably can't believe that you, of all people, got involved with such an abusive man. Maybe you saw the signs, yet you remained in the relationship in order to change him. Decide to no longer hide from your experiences as a victim of intimate partner abuse. Rather, embrace your encounters and become a more resilient survivor to take control of your entire existence. If you have somehow managed to leave the relationship, you are no longer a victim but a survivor.

If you are a friend or loved one of someone who is in an abusive relationship, you have your own challenges and frustrations with that person, and they can feel surprisingly overwhelming. One of the best things you can do is simply ask how you can be helpful.

Listen and believe. It is hard to believe that someone could actually treat another person this way. If someone is telling you about domestic violence, it is probably true. Abusers intentionally make their victims feel guilty, embarrassed, and confused. Listen openly and without judgment.

Stay in touch. Abusers frequently isolate their victims from friends and family. Do not take it personally if she is unable to see you. Do your best to stay in her life. Check in with her as often as possible, and let her know that you care.

Focus on the abuse. Point out the behaviors that are abusive, controlling, and coercive rather than criticize the abuser. Talking about what an awful person the abuser is will likely make her defensive and ultimately push her away from you.

Place blame where it belongs. The abuser does everything he can to make her feel responsible for the abuse by minimizing and placing the blame on the woman. Remember that the abuse is not her fault. No one wants or deserves to be treated in this terrible manner.

As I already mentioned, it is only too easy to think, *Why doesn't she just leave?* Sometimes it is more dangerous to leave. On the other hand, she may simply love him. Instead of being angry at her, be angry at how the abuser behaves.

Engage a safety plan. The victim knows best how to keep herself and her children safe. Ask how you can be a helpful part of their safety plan. It is also important to keep yourself safe. The abuse may be directed at your friend, but you should also consider your own safety.

Give her power and control. Domestic violence strips a victim of her power and control. Do not tell her what you think she should do. Instead, support her in making her own decisions about her current situation and her life.

Finally, we must always remember that domestic violence does not discriminate. One story will never fit all, and each story is unique. There is light at the end of the dark tunnel, and no one has to live in darkness forever. What is important is to remain resolute in taking tragedy and turning it into triumph.

CHAPTER 16

Empowering the Black Woman

I know my worth and I respect who I am as a woman.
I've got beauty on the inside and that makes me
empowered and powerful. I'm fearless and comfortable
in my own skin. I've got flaws, but I'm still confident!
—Stephanie Lahart

When all is said and done, women of color, in particular, belong to an oppressed population. Not only have they struggled, and are still struggling—with below-par education, lower-paying jobs, workplace discrimination, unaffordable housing, and confinement to a life of poverty—but they are also subjected to all manner of unspeakable abuse on the domestic front. According to Lorraine Gutierrez, Arthur F. Thurnau Professor of Psychology, Professor of Social Work, and Director of the Center for Community Learning at the University of Michigan, "Women of color experience the 'double jeopardy' of racism and sexism in American society." Professor Gutierrez is eminently qualified to make this profound pronouncement. Her research work is largely focused on empowerment theory and practice, the experiences of women of color, and multicultural organizational and community change strategies.

Women of color find themselves in abusive relationships that contribute to their struggle with feelings of helplessness, hopelessness, and powerlessness. Professor Gutierrez further explains, "Empowerment is the process of increasing personal, interpersonal, or political power so that individuals, families, and communities can take action to improve their situations."

My ultimate aim in writing this book is to suggest strategies for empowering abused women of color in the face of the harrowing challenges they face in their domestic and work lives so that they can live with dignity, self-respect, and self-worth. The empowerment model propounded by Gutierrez is highly recommended for those who work with abused Black women. She describes the four general aspects of the empowerment process as *increasing self-efficacy, developing group consciousness, reducing self-blame*, and *assuming personal responsibility for change*.

In many respects, abused Black women struggle with feelings of worthlessness. That ought not to come as the least bit of a surprise. After all, considering all the trauma visited on their self-worth, they end up blaming themselves for the abuse inflicted on them. Therapist Julian Rappaport expressed his belief in the empowerment theory by writing, "By empowerment I mean that our aim should be to enhance the possibilities for people to control their own lives." There are those who believe that empowering Black women can enhance and promote a general improvement in the quality of life among Black families. The word *empower* itself is defined as the process of making an individual stronger and more confident, especially in the vital realm of controlling their life and laying a perfectly valid claim to their rights.

There is a need for abused women to find professional help through a domestic violence (DV) advocate or counselor to embark on the laborious process of rebuilding their self-esteem and empowering themselves for a brighter future. Another effective strategy for empowering women is to design, construct, and execute domestic violence workshops for women of diverse age groups. Such workshops will include talk therapy and educational programs that will provide adequate information on the early identification of relationship red flags while also providing educational resources to support battered women. For years, DV advocates have said, "The best way to help survivors is to give them back their power and control." They are right in this submission. That is why pastors, advocates, and counselors need to integrate compassionate therapy with techniques from the empowerment model to promote psychological healing.

Based on my research, the frequent reoccurrence of intimate partner violence among African American families is due to a variety of reasons, including financial hardship, unemployment, and a lack of positive role models who can demonstrate exemplary behavior patterns in the home. My ultimate goal is to raise awareness of the vital need for workshops to educate African American church leaders, pastors, and their congregations about the dangers of domestic violence and the solutions needed to address intimate partner violence within the African American family and the church community at large. I will continue to address the issue of the apprehension of abused Black women about reporting intimate partner violence due to fear of spousal reprisal, the misguided ideology of male dominance, and poor interpersonal relationships with police departments. Other crucial subject matters that workshops should address include the lack of pastoral preparation for addressing domestic violence, the need for the creation of a safe sanctuary in the church, and the compelling need for pastors to work with social service agencies.

According to researcher Michael Friedman, those in Black church leadership are under an inalienable obligation to empower abused women. Those in clerical positions must take the leadership role in fighting against all forms of oppression, injustice, and inequality within the church. The clergy has an obligation not only to minister to the spiritual and emotional needs of abused women but must also offer a safety plan, referrals to social services and DV shelters, resources, and interventions to aid in the empowerment of these broken sisters.

It is an acknowledged fact that many African American women in abusive relationships are reluctant to dial 911 because they know that Black men, especially poor Black men, are more likely than Whites to receive harsh and often unfair treatment from the police and the court systems. This reluctance results in the underreporting of domestic violence, failing to capture the significance or prevalence of the problem of intimate partner violence. Domestic violence most often occurs in silence, and in many instances, churches are blissfully unaware that many Black families are in trouble and are being severely impacted by incidences of violence. On the obverse, many incidences of domestic violence are blatantly ignored by church leadership. Several abused Christian women, including wives of bishops, pastors, and elders, have kept their partner's abuse a secret. However, because clergy are often the first to be contacted for intervention and support, one can never overemphasize the importance of pastoral counselor training in the offering of supportive resources like empathetic psychotherapy to women who have been verbally, emotionally, and physically traumatized. As Delman L. Coates, Baptist minister and senior pastor at Mt. Enron Baptist Church, Clinton, Maryland, said, "The role of the black church is to equip those in the African American community with the tools to understand and to explain the social, political, and economic pain that they experience."

In the foreseeable future, I intend to create an empowerment program for abused women of color, in which I will be actively involved in conducting workshops, training on domestic violence, and providing empowerment tools for clergy within the Black church setting. I will also continually endeavor to highlight valuable and relevant information, with the cooperation and contribution of women whose lives have been upended by violent intimate partners. Through my work, I sincerely and fervently envisage that church leaders can and will acknowledge the cancer of intimate partner violence and the devastating impact of verbal, psychological, sexual, financial, and physical abuse on African American women in the church. It is also my sincere hope that the journey to educate and provide meaningful strategies to support and empower abused women can begin and then transform into a life-giving water well of purpose for abused partners.

The educational workshops I propose will focus on how to empower abused women within a safe setting where their voices will be heard in a non-judgmental manner so that they can receive the support they need in a therapeutic environment. It cannot be emphasized enough that the clergy must take the leadership role in fighting against all forms of oppression, injustice, and inequality within the church. These workshops will have resource persons, including mental health professionals and domestic violence advocates. Pastoral care counseling will also be provided to African American church communities. The workshops will teach that African American church leaders have the responsibility to minister to the spiritual, psychological, and emotional needs of abused women. Also, there will be education on effective ways by which church leadership and congregations can hold abusive men accountable for their abusive actions at home. Most certainly, the church can do more by offering a safe sanctuary, helping with formulating a safety plan, providing resources and interventions to aid in emotional healing, and facilitating empowerment for abused Black women.

A Wake-Up Call

Abuse and respect are diametric opposites. You
do not respect someone whom you abuse, and
you do not abuse someone whom you respect.

—Lundy Bancroft

f you are reading these words, it means you have taken the precious time to journey with me through the pages of this book. I thank you for that. Accept my sincere gratitude for making my effort a worthwhile one. The road of life can be long, arduous, and tedious. It is harder still if there is no hand to hold as you trudge along, weary from the burden of it all. The effort of writing this book was a journey in itself. By reading this book to the end, you were merely accompanying me on the journey. Thank you for holding my hand, even as I held yours, as we made the journey together.

The toughest part of overcoming trauma is forgiving oneself. If there is one final message I would like you to take away from our joint journey, it is that we must forgive ourselves and dare to set those vital boundaries that will eventually protect our personal development and advancement. Each and every day, we must meet the challenge of being better than we were yesterday. People will always be quick to judge you, especially when they have not walked in your shoes or know your story. Anytime I remember my own horrendous experience with an intimate partner in a domestic violent relationship, I am honestly grateful to be alive today, and I am humbled by the grace of God upon my life. My fervent prayer is that you will find sufficient grace not only to survive domestic abuse but also to become an advocate in the fight against this terrible domestic malignancy.

The 2023 report from the New York City Domestic Fatality Review Committee is a stark wake-up call. Intimate partner violence surged by a harrowing 29 percent between 2021 and 2022, making it the second-largest increase in a decade. This crisis demands our immediate attention, and we cannot afford to remain silent any longer. Although New York City is being cast in the mold of the safest mega-metropolis globally, this is not the reality for those living through the horrors of intimate partner violence. The shocking 29 percent increase in intimate partner fatalities between 2021 and 2022 is not a mere statistic. It is a devastating reality that ought to numb our sensibilities that we all rise up to confront it headlong. Despite progress in reducing other forms of homicides, intimate partner homicides persist, escalating by a staggering 225 percent in Brooklyn alone, and 57 percent in the Bronx during the same period.

This surge in intimate partner homicides continues to disproportionately impact Black and Hispanic women from marginalized communities. Therefore, it requires solutions tailored to meet the peculiar needs of these often-overlooked populations. The statistics speak volumes. Black women, constituting only 21 percent of New York City's population, account for a staggering 41 percent of intimate partner homicides. Safety can never be negotiable, regardless of race, socio-economic status, or gender identity. Our cities must start implementing a targeted public education and awareness campaign with a focus on communities of color, designed to empower Black women, especially church leaders, to identify the signs of abuse and where abused females can seek help.

To ultimately eradicate domestic violence from the root, there needs to be a unified effort by various social services agencies, educators, and women organizations, as well as church leadership collaborating with pastoral counselors, domestic violence advocacy groups, and local government leaders. This collaboration should work to not only implement changes in cultures that create, reinforce, and potentiate domestic violence but also organize and lobby legislative systems to better address domestic violence. There may be a need to call attention to behaviors and comments that degrade women and support violence. Within society, we frequently hear excuses made, for example, "boys will be boys," in response to boys acting in harmful ways that normalize the behavior. Instead of ignoring violence, aggression, and a lack of empathy, parents, teachers, and pastors can teach boys alternatives and hold them accountable in ways that allow them to learn from their mistakes and make amends. One critical way of confronting the mindset that normalizes domestic violence is by educating young people to grow up believing that love, equality, and respect are fundamental biblical principles and providing guidelines for expectations of how to treat females with compassion and empathy. Leaders need to encourage schools to include violence prevention education across all grade levels. Pastors must have honest conversations on the dynamics of domestic violence. Abusive people must be held accountable for their violent behaviors. Individuals who perpetrate domestic violence usually do not see themselves as being abusive because more often these individuals, mostly men, minimize their violent behaviors.

When church leaders invest intentionally in the detection, reduction, and prevention of intimate partner violence, focusing on all families and community-based strategies, it results in tangible reductions in domestic violence. Leadership, as well as members in churches, must remain unwavering with a strong commitment to ending the abusive cycles that fuel intimate partner violence. I use the pages of this book to call on the authorities to prioritize investments in violence prevention and holistic community solutions to end domestic violence. We have the tools, the knowledge, and the will to put an end to domestic violence. In her widely acclaimed book *No Visible Bruises: What We Don't Know About Domestic Violence Can Kill Us*, Rachel Louise Snyder writes, "Not having a national conversation about domestic violence is a problem. We need to make space for everyone to talk about their experiences with it, whether you're a woman, man, child or non-heteronormative person. What I hear from advocates is it's hearing the stories firsthand that change minds.

We need to make space for those stories to be heard." Rachel Snyder is right. Domestic violence is a public health crisis and a social delinquent that truly does thrive in silence, and bringing public awareness and education that this can happen to anyone is truly the first step in ending this pervasive silent issue.

Boys who see their fathers and other men abuse women are more likely to be abusive. We see men using violence in our media habitually that it seems normal. Using violence, manipulation, and dominance is a learned behavior and a choice. Domestic violence is not caused by mental illness or substance abuse, although certain substances do enhance violent tendencies within some individuals. Additionally, there is a need for programs that will educate men about the behaviors they learned, hold them accountable, and help them make different decisions. We must shift the culture that supports domestic violence. Many stereotypes about masculinity normalize gender-based violence against women and children. As we become more aware of how power dynamics are learned, we are better able as individuals and communities to notice, point out, and do the work to eliminate the underpinnings of violence. In other words, we can all demand accountability and equality to end domestic violence.

In conclusion, I will close with a word for pastors and church leaders. David G. Benner is an internationally renowned clinical psychologist, author, and wisdom teacher. He wrote, "Pastoral counseling involves the establishment of a time-limited relationship that is structured to provide comfort for troubled persons by enhancing their awareness of God's grace." Therapy provides insight. It also enhances and promotes the ability of hurting individuals to work through trauma and live a more balanced life. In that regard, Dr. Benner further articulates, "The ministry of pastoral care and counseling presents a unique opportunity for God's Word to be articulated by pastors and Bible teachers. Pastoral counseling fulfills one's calling to be a minister of the Word and in services for the care of the soul."

The overriding obligation of pastors as they listen to abused women is to provide emotional support and therapeutic treatment. Pastors can benefit from gaining more knowledge from books relating to social issues like the impact of poverty on women of color, racial injustice, gender inequality, managing grief, and marriage counseling. Pastoral care is obliged to unconditionally offer a safe environment in which not only abused women of color but females from all cultural backgrounds can receive empathetic and compassionate treatment. Finally, I call on pastors and all in church leadership to reach out to the many battered Christian women who are experiencing psychological brokenness, feelings of helplessness, and disempowerment and who are suffering heartache and injuries in various forms, and to connect with them to offer pastoral care and counseling in a respectful, empathetic, and nonjudgmental attitude.

Finally, let me say a word of prayer for all women who are suffering at this very moment from verbal, psychological, sexual, and physical traumas of intimate partner violence from a verse from 1 of the Psalmist David's prayers: "In my desperation I prayed, and the Lord listened; he saved me from all my troubles" (Psalm 34:6 NLT).

God bless you all.

Sonia Martin
Mount Vernon, New York,
United States of America
June 2024

ABOUT THE AUTHOR

Sonia Martin was born in Kingston, Jamaica, West Indies and she migrated to the United States of America over forty years ago. She is a graduate of New York University NYC, where she obtained a master's degree in social work. She has a master's degree in pastoral care and counseling from New York Theological Seminary in New York City. Sonia Martin obtained a doctor of ministry degree from Northeastern Seminary at Roberts Wesleyan University located in Rochester, New York. Sonia Martin has been actively involved in church ministry for more than forty-five years.